# ROOTED

## 52-WEEK BIBLE READING PLAN + STUDY GUIDE

## VOLUME 2

### ROOTED MOMS MINISTRIES
*WITH KATIE GIBSON AND OTHER CONTRIBUTORS*

ISBN 9798840312704

**EDITORIAL TEAM**
Katie Gibson | Founder & Executive Director, Rooted Moms Ministries
Brooke Parker | Editor, Rooted Moms Devotional Writer Team

**DEVOTIONAL WRITER TEAM**

Lonette Baity | www.lonettebaity.com
Debbie Burns
Jannetta Cox | jsamobucox.wordpress.com
Nancy Ehlinger | nancyehlinger.wordpress.com
Wendy Gerdes | www.wendygerdes.com
Katie Gibson | www.katiegibsonwrites.com
Heather Kenny | www.leadingfromthedeepend.com
Brenna Kurz
Joan Lavori
Brittany Marlow
Lindsay McNeely
Tierney Nashleanas

Jessica Parker
Audra Powers
Jess Ridgeway
Renee Robinson | www.renee-robinson.com
Martha Rudolph | www.martharudolph.weebly.com
Dana Schaefer
Breanna Faith Spearman
Keryn Stokes
Taylor Watkins
Saretta Wells | onepassionatemommi.wixsite.com/beloved-1/blog
Kristen Williamson

**BOOK DESIGN**
Katie Gibson | Founder & Executive Director, Rooted Moms Ministries

# CONTENTS

About Rooted Moms | 5

About Our Plan | 6

How to Use This Study | 7

Before You Begin: Note to Self | 8

## OLD TESTAMENT

**Old Testament R.O.O.T. Journaling Guide | 9**

Week One | 10

Week Two | 14

Week Three | 18

Week Four | 22

Week Five | 26

**Quiet Time Guide | 30**

Week Six | 32

Week Seven | 36

Week Eight | 40

Week Nine | 44

Week Ten | 48

**How to Study the Bible | 52**

Week Eleven | 54

Week Twelve | 58

Week Thirteen | 62

Week Fourteen | 66

Week Fifteen | 70

**When Quiet Time Isn't Quiet | 74**

Week Sixteen | 76

Week Seventeen | 80

Week Eighteen | 84

Week Nineteen | 88

Week Twenty | 92

Week Twenty-One | 96

**Major & Minor Prophets R.O.O.T. Journaling Guide | 100**

Week Twenty-Two | 101

Week Twenty-Three | 105

Week Twenty-Four | 109

Week Twenty-Five | 113

**Write Your Story | 117**

Week Twenty-Six | 120

Week Twenty-Seven | 124

Week Twenty-Eight | 128

Week Twenty-Nine | 132

## NEW TESTAMENT

**The Gospels R.O.O.T. Journaling Guide | 136**

Week Thirty | 137

Week Thirty-One | 141

Week Thirty-Two | 145

**Prayer Guide | 149**

Week Thirty-Three | 153

Week Thirty-Four | 157

Week Thirty-Five | 161

Week Thirty-Six | 165

**Acts & Epistles R.O.O.T. Journaling Guide | 169**

Week Thirty-Seven | 170

Week Thirty-Eight | 174

Week Thirty-Nine | 178

Week Forty | 182

Week Forty-One | 186

Week Forty-Two | 190

Week Forty-Three | 194

**Better Together | 198**

Week Forty-Four |200

Week Forty-Five | 204

Week Forty-Six | 208

Week Forty-Seven | 212

Week Forty-Eight | 216

Week Forty-Nine | 220

Week Fifty | 224

Week Fifty-One | 228

Week Fifty-Two | 232

**Celebrate | 236**

What Now? | 238

Connect with Rooted Moms | 239

# ABOUT
# ROOTED MOMS

**Rooted Moms** is a non-profit non-denominational Christian ministry that exists to help moms thrive in every season of life by becoming rooted in Christ (Col. 2:7), growing in God's Word (Ps. 1:1-3), and gathering in life-giving community (Heb. 10:24-25).

We believe the abundant life we long for is achieved not by striving harder, but by abiding more deeply in Christ. We believe the influence of a mom cannot be overstated— when we invest in spiritually strong moms, we reap spiritually strong marriages, families, churches, and communities.

Our operations team is made up of moms who desire to share what we've experienced: the life-changing power of being rooted in Jesus. We provide free resources, community, and encouragement that help moms grow in their relationship with Christ, and more fully experience a life of fulfillment and freedom in Him.

At the heart of Rooted Moms are our online small groups where women from around the world meet weekly to connect and grow in our faith. Together, we are getting to know Jesus through His Word, and experiencing the power of doing life together. Rooted Moms groups are open to women from all different stages of life. **Visit www.rootedmoms.com to learn more and connect with our online community.**

# ABOUT
# OUR PLAN

**The Rooted & Growing Bible reading plan** is a chronological, 52-week, 5-days per week reading plan that covers a comprehensive portion of the Old Testament, and nearly every chapter of the New Testament.

**Why are there missing chapters in the reading plan?** We believe that having a practical plan that works for your season of life is one of the most important keys to establishing a consistent quiet time. As busy moms, we love the 2-3 chapters per day, five days per week schedule format because it leaves plenty of time for catch-up when *life happens!*

While, yes, we believe that the entire Bible is God-breathed and useful for equipping believers (2 Tim. 3:16-17), our Rooted and Growing Bible reading plan highlights foundational passages of Scripture. Our goal is to lead women to know and trust God more deeply through His Word, by better understanding the big picture of the Gospel.

The majority of the Old Testament passages not included fall in one of these categories:
1. They are lists of numbers, genealogical records, or requirements for offerings and purification (laws).
2. They are duplicate passages, already covered in a previous day's reading.
3. They are Psalms and Proverbs. While there are a few key chapters included, the majority are not simply because these are books we tend to naturally gravitate to when reading God's Word. We encourage you to incorporate a chapter or two from these books into your weekly routine, on the weekend, or when you're looking for additional reading.

Our community begins reading the plan together each September, however you can start at any time that works for your schedule! If you choose to study along, be sure to subscribe to our weekly emails for additional free resources. You can also join one of our online community groups for ongoing accountability, care, and connection. You can jump in with us at any point however if you want to start from Genesis visit www.rootedmoms.com/grow to see when our new year will begin.

**For our team's favorite study resources, visit www.rootedmoms.com/study**

# HOW TO USE THIS STUDY

**What you will need:**
- A Bible
- A pen
- A highlighter
- A journal

**For each week of our reading study, you will find:**
- A 5-day Bible reading plan
- A key memory verse
- A corresponding Devotional
- A journaling Page to record your key takeaways

**Scripture is the core of our study.** Schedule five days per week to listen to or read the assigned passages and study through them using the provided R.O.O.T. journaling guide. (The other two days can be used for catch-up, or reading additional Scripture not covered in the plan!)

**Memorize the key verse** using our FREE online resources. Don't just get in Scripture— get Scripture *in you!*

**The devotionals are what we call the "cherry on top," and expound on each week's reading.** Written by moms, for moms, they cover a wide range of topics from trusting God with our children to enduring hardship— and everything in between!

**At the end of the week, take a few extra minutes to reflect and record your most compelling takeaway.** Has the way you view yourself or God changed? Is there an action you are committing to take? How did God speak to you through His Word this week? Jot it down to record your journey through the Word.

**Life is better together.** Studying God's Word is no exception. Ask a friend (or five!) to study along with you (see our "Better Together" resource on page 198 to learn more).

# NOTE TO SELF

At Rooted Moms we always say, "God meets us at our level of expectation."

So today, as you begin this year-long adventure of knowing Christ more deeply through His Word, consider this question: **What do I expect from my time in the Word this year?**

Is your aim to *finally* establish a consistent quiet time?
Do you desire to gain a better understanding of the big picture of the Gospel?
Are you longing for spiritual strength and stability?
Is your goal to memorize and internalize more Scripture?

Use the space below to write a note to yourself, that you'll re-visit at the end of the year. Write down your expectations, your hopes, and even your apprehensions. Cast a vision for where you see yourself a year from now. If you need more space, write your "note to self" in your personal journal.

*Expect big things, friend.*

_____

_____

_____

_____

_____

_____

_____

_____

_____

_____

_____

_____

_____

_____

_____

# R.O.O.T.

## JOURNALING GUIDE

It's one thing to read God's Word; it's another thing to actually *understand* and *apply* it.

Move from information to practical application with our tried-and-true R.O.O.T. study method. Use your journal to walk through the following steps for each day's reading:

### READ

Read the passage of Scripture, highlighting or underlining any words or phrases that stick out to you.

### OWN WORDS

Shorten the overall story or message into your own words.

### OBSERVE

Jot down your observations. Here are some questions to get you started—
- What part of today's reading stood out to you the most, and why?
- What does this passage reveal about God's character?
- Is there a person in today's reading whose actions and character prefigure Jesus?
- What verse(s) encouraged you? What verse(s) challenged you?
- Was there anything you didn't understand?*

### TAKEAWAY

What is God prompting you to do? Write down one way you can apply the truth(s) you learned to your life today.
- Is there a sin of which you need to repent?
- Is there a person you need to forgive?
- Is there a fear you need to confront?
- Is there a truth you need to believe?
- Is there a command you need to obey?

*We love the Enduring Word Commentary for all those hard-to-understand moments in Scripture!
Visit www.enduringword.com or download the app for quick and easy access.*

# 1

## WEEK ONE

### *LIGHT*

GENESIS 1-2

GENESIS 3-4

GENESIS 6-7

GENESIS 8-9

JOB 1-2

**MEMORY VERSE**

"WHEN JESUS SPOKE AGAIN TO THE PEOPLE, HE SAID,
'I AM THE LIGHT OF THE WORLD. WHOEVER FOLLOWS
ME WILL NEVER WALK IN DARKNESS, BUT WILL HAVE
THE LIGHT OF LIFE.'"

**JOHN 8:12**

# LET THERE BE LIGHT

**BY DANA SCHAEFER**

"Mommy, my lightflash doesn't work," wailed my five-year old son as he frantically pushed the button in and out on his tiny blue flashlight. I suppressed a giggle at his precious word reversal and helped him get new batteries to make the light reappear for him. Proudly, he waved his "lightflash" around the room like a Jedi yielding a lightsaber, happy that it worked and gave off a strong, bright beam.

Remembering this moment, I recalled other times that light became important in my children's lives. Fondly, I recalled the necessary glow of the nightlight in an infant's nursery to help me change dirty diapers or wet crib sheets while I was half-asleep. That same nightlight lit an anxious toddler's room as she learned to sleep in a big bed alone. Tangles of Christmas lights encircle our living room as we wind them around the tree each November, just before the magical moment when the tree twinkles and ushers in holiday cheer.

There have been campfires complete with sticky s'mores and friends laughing and sharing stories. I remember sleepovers with the lights on way too late into the night to celebrate the burgeoning independence of older children. I imagine at some point in the future, the flicker of candles will set the mood for romantic dinners or perhaps even wedding ceremonies when my children move into a new phase of their lives. When each distinct light shines, a season in my motherhood journey becomes discernible in its radiance.

God has used light to mark the passage of time and to govern days and nights since the very beginning—or at least since the fourth day. He didn't use little pink or blue candles to mark the passage of years like we do on birthday cakes. Nevertheless He used lights, astronomically big ones: the sun, moon, and stars. Genesis 1:14 says, "And God said, 'Let there be lights in the vault of the sky to separate the day from the night, and let them serve as signs to mark sacred times, and days and years.'"

God knew the power light would have and thought it was the right way to separate the night from the day, and to mark units of time as distinct, special, and unique. This verse even describes these units of time as "sacred." God chose light because He is light. From the first chapter of the Bible, we see how foundational light is to faith. Not only does God use light to mark times and seasons, He himself is the light that illuminates the darkness.

> "Look for God's light to guide you through the dark moments."

No matter where you are on your motherhood journey, you already know that there are sacred moments built into this gig. Some of the sacred moments are the hardest ones, the ones when it is easy to feel alone and hidden in darkness as you go through them.

When you hit those bumpy patches, remember God is there with you. **Look for God's light to guide you through the dark moments.** He sees your tears, hears your prayers, and offers His comfort and peace to you in a way only He can.

When your heart feels full to bursting with pride and love for your child, remember God's graciousness as He entrusted you to be the mom for your child. As the days, years, and seasons roll by, be assured that the very God who created night and day also empowers you to do the holy work of motherhood. Walk with Him and savor the sacred seasons, trusting His light to guide the way.

# 2

## WEEK TWO

### *HUMILITY*

JOB 3, 4:1-8, 5:17-27

JOB 6:1-17, 32:1-3, 38

JOB 40, 42

GENESIS 11-12

GENESIS 13-14

## MEMORY VERSE

"BUT HE GIVES US MORE GRACE. THAT IS WHY
SCRIPTURE SAYS: 'GOD OPPOSES THE PROUD BUT
SHOWS FAVOR TO THE HUMBLE.'"

**JAMES 4:6**

# FACE THE GRACE

**BY TAYLOR WATKINS**

"I'm an alcoholic," I admitted to my therapist. I had held this in for quite some time.

How silly does that sound? I wanted to hide this from a person whose job is literally to help me with my mental health. I wanted to keep that skeleton tucked away, pretending it wasn't a problem because in all honesty, I hated drinking. It was making me miserable but when I had thoughts that wouldn't stop, when my anxiety took over, I turned to alcohol instead of God. I realized I had also been avoiding God. I felt guilty praying because I knew I was sinning.

Job also admitted some really awful ideas and thoughts to His Heavenly Father. One of the most heart wrenching parts of his dialogue is when he tells God he wishes he was never born. Yet God wasn't surprised and He didn't turn away.

Job was concentrated on the why: "Why me? Why now? Why, why, why?" God's response wasn't what Job expected, but rather answered his question with "Who are you?" God didn't belittle Job and his despair, but rather realigned his perspective. When we are completely vulnerable with our God, we are able to fully see what God is trying to tell us. Our hearts are changed.

God already knows how you feel whether you share your feelings or not. God turns the table and begins to ask Job some hard questions, some things we still don't have the answers to. Job responds with a change of heart: "Then Job replied to the Lord: 'I know that you can do all things; no purpose of yours can be thwarted. You asked, "Who is this that obscures my plans without knowledge?" Surely I spoke of things I did not understand, things too wonderful for me to know'" (Job 42:1-3).

In this conversation between God and Job, we start to understand that we aren't meant to lean on our own understanding, but to trust in the Lord. God made it clear to Job that he failed to do this.

But I have to believe that even though Job had to swallow this hard truth, he was comforted knowing that he didn't have to pretend in front of his Heavenly Father. That by being vulnerable, God spoke truth over him. **Vulnerability leads to humility which softens our hearts to truth.** He may not give you the response you want, but He will always give you the truth.

Shortly after the conversation with my therapist, I came to God and I admitted I was weak. I needed Him to battle with me and sustain me. I needed Him to fight these intrusive thoughts because He has strength I never will. I am not close to perfect; I never will be. But I can say alcohol doesn't control my life anymore and those intrusive thoughts are getting better and better with every prayer and Christ-centered person He continues to place in my life. I could sum it all up to this: His grace.

Sister, what question are you struggling with today? Whether it's an addiction, an illness you feel is unfair, a circumstance you feel you can't bear, be honest and bring it to His feet today. Pour out your heart and ugly truth. Listen for God's loving response and pour into His word. You don't have to fake it or hide; He will love you through it. He will love you because of it. He will restore you, not through your power, but His power and His perfect love in your weakness.

"Vulnerability leads to humility which softens our hearts to truth."

# 3

## WEEK THREE

### *COMPROMISE*

GENESIS 15-16

GENESIS 17-18

GENESIS 19-20

GENESIS 21-22

GENESIS 23-24

## MEMORY VERSE

"BLESSED ARE THOSE WHOSE WAYS ARE BLAMELESS,
WHO WALK ACCORDING TO THE LAW OF THE LORD."

**PSALM 119:1**

# CAMPING IN COMPROMISE

**BY KATIE GIBSON**

I helped lower my friend to the bed, as she stammered in her drunken state. The party we were at had gotten out of hand. Things were said that couldn't be unheard, and actions that couldn't be undone. "It's okay," I said to her, stuffing my hurt down deeper.

I woke up with a physical and emotional hangover, as those hurt feelings rose back to the surface. Internally I lamented, *How did things end up like this?*

I wonder if Lot asked the same way as he walked away from smoldering Sodom. I wonder if he reflected on the events that had left him wife-less and homeless. How did this nephew of Abram (who had been rescued once before, by the way) end up in this situation where he barely escaped utter destruction?

If we look closely at Lot's journey, we can see a progression:
He *encamped* near Sodom (Gen. 13:10-13).
He *lived in* Sodom (Gen. 14:12).
He *became a leader of* Sodom (Gen. 19:1).

I would wager that Lot wished he could go back and reverse his choice to live near the infamously wicked city of Sodom. At the time, Lot had reasoned his decision— anyone in their right mind would choose a lush, well-watered plain over one that is rocky and arid.

If I look closely at my own journey, I recognize a similar pattern. I reasoned that the good land of acceptance was better than the alternative loneliness. I encamped near places of sin, and it wasn't long before I found myself living in compromise. Even then I reasoned, "At least I'm not as bad as so-and-so." Eventually, with little self-awareness, I became a well-established member of the "city."

**Reasoning is a slippery slope that leads us to desolate places of compromise.** Can you think of a situation, past or present, in your life, that left you spiritually impoverished and full of regrets?

# "Reasoning is a slippery slope that leads us to desolate places of compromise."

We all face situations where we are tempted to reason a less-than-ideal decision. So how do we avoid the pitfall of settling? Read the following verses from Psalm 1:1-3 where we see a familiar progression. Pay special attention, in the middle, to the psalmist's prescribed escape plan:

"Blessed is the one who does not *walk* in step with the wicked or *stand* in the way that sinners take or *sit in* the company of mockers, but whose *delight is in the law of the Lord, and who meditates on his law day and night.* That person is like a tree planted by streams of water, which yields its fruit in season and whose leaf does not wither— whatever they do prospers" (Ps. 1:1-3, emphasis added).

Did you catch it? The antidote to reasoning is wisdom found in the Word of God. When we commit ourselves to delight in, meditate on, and obey God's instructions, we set ourselves up for a life of abundance.

Stop right now and take note of any areas of compromise in your life—

A friendship with someone of the opposite sex
A television show that is less-than-kosher
A group of co-workers you eat lunch with who spread rumors and gossip

Whether you're encamped near, living in, or a leader in any place of sin, it's never too late to turn from your ways and turn back to God's again.

Take the hand of Jesus, and *run*. Don't look back, friend. Make a plan to get in the Word of God, and make it the ultimate authority in your life. Don't tolerate that old friend, Reason, anymore and you will find your life, in time, flourishing once again.

# 4

## WEEK FOUR

### QUESTIONS

GENESIS 25-26

GENESIS 27-28

GENESIS 29-30

GENESIS 31-32

GENESIS 33-34

## MEMORY VERSE

"'CALL TO ME AND I WILL ANSWER YOU AND
TELL YOU GREAT AND UNSEARCHABLE THINGS
YOU DO NOT KNOW.'"

**JEREMIAH 33:3**

# GOD QUESTIONS?

**BY LONETTE M. BAITY**

Have you ever been in conversation with a three-year-old? My little one is constantly asking questions about people, places and random things and she is relentless:

*"Mama, where are we going?*
*Why are goin 'der?*
*Can I go wit' you?*

It's hilarious and exhausting. What I love about her is she asks with her heart wide open and full of faith knowing I will have an answer for her even if it isn't the answer she's expecting.

In Genesis 25, it seems Rebekah has a similar idea. We see Isaac cry out to God for his wife to be able to conceive. The Lord answers by blessing Rebekah with twins. But the twins struggle so fiercely in her womb that it causes her much pain and agony. (I remember my son using my insides for soccer practice; I felt like he was trying to escape through my rib cage! I can't imagine having two babies fighting. Poor Rebekah!)

Rebekah wants to know *why*. So she takes her question to the only One who can answer it. What I love is that God doesn't criticize her for asking. He doesn't say, "I'm sovereign. Deal with it!" Like a good father, he shares his heart with her. In Genesis 25:22-23, God takes her question and gives her a promise. As we read Rebekah's story and how it unfolds throughout a generation, we can see God's presence and providence.

Like He did for Rebekah, **God exchanges our questions for promises loaded with exactly what we need to endure.** He promises to be our provision even when we endure times of lack. He promises to be present with us even in times of trouble and more.

> "God exchanges our questions for promises loaded with exactly what we need to endure."

In my own life, I'm trying to be a little more like my three-year-old. I'm learning to take my questions to The Father with an open heart. It's a dialogue with him that deepens our relationship. He gives me insight into His heart. He recalibrates my heart to his sovereignty, kindness, and providence in every circumstance ... even if it means I don't get the answer I was expecting.

Take some time this week to take your *why* to The Father. Let it spark a conversation where He refreshes your hope and shows you His character. Even if He doesn't give the answer you want, He will answer. Use your journal to record your conversation with Him. You can come back to those answers when you need encouragement or clarity.

# 5

## WEEK FIVE

### *LOOK*

GENESIS 35, 37

GENESIS 38-39

GENESIS 40-41

GENESIS 42-43

GENESIS 44-45

**MEMORY VERSE**

"THE LORD IS RIGHTEOUS IN ALL HIS WAYS AND FAITHFUL IN ALL HE DOES. THE LORD IS NEAR TO ALL WHO CALL ON HIM, TO ALL WHO CALL ON HIM IN TRUTH."

**PSALM 145:17-18**

# LOOKING FOR GOD

**BY JESS RIDGEWAY**

Have you noticed that when you buy a new car and take it home, you begin to see that car everywhere? Or when you finally take the plunge on a new pair of jeans you've been eyeing at Target – suddenly everyone and your mom are wearing them?

We recently upgraded our family vehicle. The first time I drove it to the park, a parade of similar models pulled in right behind me. Apparently gray SUVs are the membership card of millennial mamas everywhere. High five to you if you're in the club! Those new things that were once a novelty, the car and the jeans, become familiar and all of a sudden you start to spot them everywhere.

As we're nearing the end of Genesis, Joseph steps onto the scene. So far, we've seen God begin to fulfill two of his promises to Abraham, to have a land and a family. Now, in the Joseph saga we'll see the first glimpses of this family becoming a blessing to the nations. But in order to get there, Joseph is going to endure some hard years. He'll be betrayed, sold into slavery, set up, put in prison, and forgotten. It seems like he just can't catch a break.

And yet, if we look at the details of this story, we see God clearly at work:
- Joseph was wandering to find his brothers and "by chance" was given directions by a stranger (Gen. 37:15).
- Two of his jealous brothers have ideas that keep Joseph from death (Gen. 37:22, 26).
- He is bought and granted favor in the house of a prominent Egyptian (Gen. 39:1).
- In withstanding the advances of his master's wife, Joseph is falsely accused and imprisoned – but not executed (Gen. 39:20).
- In prison, Joseph again is granted favor and connects with one of Pharaoh's officers who will eventually recommend him to interpret Pharaoh's disturbing dream (Gen. 39: 21, 40:13, 41: 9-13).
- Giving all the credit to God, Joseph interprets the dream, offers wise counsel on how to proceed, and is given a title, prestige, and honor (Gen. 41:14-44).

We could easily attribute some of these happenings to Joseph's determination, integrity, and hard work. Some, we could say, were the evil works of others, and some sheer coincidence. But what if we gave God the credit? God doesn't deal in coincidence or serendipity; He works in providence and sovereignty. Even in the midst of the hard, behind the scenes God's hand is all over Joseph's story. His hand is all over history. Sister, His hand is all over your story, too. And what a relief it is to know that God is walking through this life by your side.

As you are going about your life, look for Him. **The more we look for God, the more we will see Him.** Just like that car or pair of jeans, He becomes familiar and we begin to spot His handprints everywhere. Take a hard look at your story. Dig into your history. Can you see Him? Can you catch a glimpse of the creator of the universe at work in your life even amidst your biggest struggles? What about today, moment by moment? Do you see Him providing you with the strength to get up in the morning, with the ability to speak kindness to your children, with peace as you make decisions for your family?

If you are having trouble finding Him, pray for that insight. Ask a friend or spouse to help. Grab your journal and write it down. May God reveal Himself to you today and may you find wonder, and peace knowing He is near and that He cares for you.

"The more we look for God, the more we will see Him."

# QUIET TIME GUIDE
*making the most of your minutes*

**God's Word helps us know Him more, and grow stronger spiritually.** That's why every minute spent in God's Word is valuable— whether it's five or fifty.

Use this scalable quiet time guide to make the most of your time, no matter the season of life you're in.

**(5)** 

## WHEN YOU HAVE FIVE MINUTES

**Listen** to the assigned Scriptures while you...
- Get ready for the day
- Nurse your baby
- Drive to work
- Wait in carline
- Tidy the house
- Stretch

**Reflect** | Sit and reflect on the following questions in your journal or notes app in your phone (3 minutes):
- What did today's reading reveal about God's character?
- What action is God asking you to take based on what you learned today?

**Pray** | Tell God one thing you are grateful for, and one specific area you need His help today (2 minutes).

**(15)**

## WHEN YOU HAVE FIFTEEN MINUTES

**Read** the assigned scriptures via a physical Bible or a Bible app (5 minutes).

**Reflect** | Use our R.O.O.T. Journaling guide to process and apply what you have read (5 minutes).

**Pray** | Thank God for who He is and what He's done. Confess any sins that have been revealed through the truth of God's Word. Cast any anxieties you woke up with on God and leave them in His trustworthy hands. Sit in silence, listening for His voice. Journal anything He speaks to you (5 minutes).

# WHEN YOU HAVE THIRTY MINUTES

**Read** the assigned scriptures via a physical Bible or the Bible app, in your favorite translation. Highlight any passages that stick out to you, and re-read them in the Amplified version (10 minutes).

**Reflect** | Use our R.O.O.T. journaling guide to process and apply what you have read (10 minutes).

**Pray** | Thank God for who He is and what He's done. Confess any sins that have been revealed through the truth of God's Word. Cast any anxieties you woke up with on God and leave them in His trustworthy hands. Sit in silence, listening for His voice. Journal anything He speaks to you (10 minutes).

> BUT GROW IN THE GRACE AND KNOWLEDGE OF OUR LORD AND SAVIOR JESUS CHRIST. TO HIM BE GLORY BOTH NOW AND FOREVER! AMEN.
>
> **2 PETER 3:18**

# WHEN YOU HAVE SIXTY MINUTES

**Read** the assigned scriptures via a physical Bible or the Bible app, in your favorite translation. Highlight any passages that stick out to you, and re-read them using the Amplified version (20 minutes).

**Reflect** | Utilize a commentary (such as Enduring Word, available via app or at www.enduringword.com) to dig deeper into the cultural and historical context behind the passages. Jot down your observations using our R.O.O.T. journaling guide. Process and apply the scripture to your everyday life, and record your key takeaway (30 minutes).

**Pray** | Thank God for who He is and what He's done. Confess any sins that have been revealed through the truth of God's Word. Cast any anxieties you woke up with on God and leave them in His trustworthy hands. Sit in silence, listening for His voice. Journal anything He speaks to you (10 minutes).

# 6

## WEEK SIX

### PLAN

GENESIS 46-47

GENESIS 48-49

GENESIS 50, EXODUS 1

EXODUS 2-3

EXODUS 4-5

**MEMORY VERSE**

"AND THE GOD OF ALL GRACE, WHO CALLED YOU TO
HIS ETERNAL GLORY IN CHRIST, AFTER YOU HAVE
SUFFERED A LITTLE WHILE, WILL HIMSELF RESTORE
YOU AND MAKE YOU STRONG, FIRM AND STEADFAST."

**1 PETER 5:10**

# GOD'S PLAN

**BY MARTHA RUDOLPH**

Do you ever feel trapped by God's plan?

Moving to Georgia was the right thing to do. It was clear that God was calling us to go, so we packed up and went.

The move was challenging, but good. We learned the area, found our people and even began checking out local churches. I found purpose as a stay-at-home-mom, serving with a local Bible study program and upkeeping our home. Life was good.

Our season of plenty lasted 4 years. In 2011 everything seemed to go wrong. Year by year our life of green pastures turned to one of hardship, disbelief and fear.

I think the Isrealites experienced similar emotional upheaval. They were minding their own business when, without chastisement or explanation, their status changed from a people privileged to despised (Exod. 1:8-14). Though the burden on the Israelites intensified, God, as promised, continued to expand their numbers, but as their population grew, so did their oppression.

Did the Israelites ever wonder what they had done to bring such a heavy burden upon themselves? Did they question their worth? Their purpose? The why of it?

We know God had a plan for Israel and it began with a boy named Moses.

But, I wasn't Moses. God wasn't calling me to stage an exodus or address a nation. Honestly, I didn't know what to do anymore. I felt lost and trapped. Tethered to a circumstance out of my control. Although I knew God was working, I just wanted out. I wonder if any Israelite felt the same?

I didn't understand it, but God had everything in His hand and just as He grew Israel into a great nation under the oppression of Pharaoh, He was at work in my heart, growing me towards spiritual maturity.

# "Circumstantial change does not cancel our calling."

It was my mindset, not my situation that had me trapped. I had been so conditioned to relate my success to my actions, that I didn't know how to be at peace with my role when everything around me was coming undone.

I was, like the Israelites, in a situation outside of my control. However, God is always in control, and He used an external circumstance to free me from an internal prison.

So friends, listen up and repeat after me: **Circumstantial change does not cancel our calling.**

The role of Israel as a nation did not change because of their oppression. They remained God's people. Called to Him. Grown through oppression into a great nation. *God always has a plan.*

I wish I had realized sooner that being trapped in God's plan is a good place to be. It is where He grows us. Where He is demonstrates His love in miraculous ways and where He frees us from burdens we were never meant to carry.

It was a lie that I had lost my calling. The way I related to it shifted, but my purpose had not. God's plan was for an internal change to allow me to fulfill my calling in a deeper way. In His wisdom, He taught me that lesson in the middle of our hardship.

If you feel trapped in His plan, let me encourage you to go to God in prayer and ask Him if there is something internal from which He is trying to set you free, and allow Him access to break the bonds. Shift your thinking and choose to live in the freedom that is God's plan.

# 7

## WEEK SEVEN

### ORIGINAL

EXODUS 6-7

EXODUS 8-9

EXODUS 10-11

EXODUS 12-13

EXODUS 14-15

**MEMORY VERSE**

"NO ONE IS LIKE YOU, LORD; YOU ARE GREAT, AND
YOUR NAME IS MIGHTY IN POWER."

**JEREMIAH 10:6**

# THE ORIGINAL

**BY DEBBIE BURNS**

Growing up, the original seamstress in our family was my Mom. She sewed flawlessly. Rarely did I wear anything before the age of thirteen that my Mom did not sew for me. She made the whole process look easy from cutting the pattern to hand stitching the hem. I watched her sew garments from start to finish countless times. I was always proud to wear a garment sewn by my Mom.

In freshman Home Ec. class, it was my turn to sew. Having watched my Mom so many times, I expected to create the same impeccable garments as my Mom. Nope! That was not the result. Much to my utter dismay, the teacher held up my garment for the class to see as an example of how terribly crooked a zipper could be, if not sewn properly. I'm mortified to say the teacher didn't stop there. On the front of my garment was an admittedly poor attempt at sewing trim on the center seam. Oh, my! I'd love to say that I, too, sewed flawlessly like my Mom, but I was a poor imitation of the original seamstress.

God is truly "The Original." He wanted Egyptians and Israelites to know "that I am the Lord" (Exod. 7:17). He wanted them all to witness the powerful works of His hands and acknowledge that only He was God. To accomplish this, God caused several plagues in Egypt before the Israelites were freed from their bonds of slavery.

When Moses and his brother, Aaron, first approached Pharaoh, God told Aaron to throw down his staff in front of Pharaoh and it would become a serpent. Pharaoh's magicians imitated this and their staffs became serpents. Since God is "The Original," Aaron's staff swallowed up all of their poor imitations (Exod. 7:9-12).

However, the imitations of "The Original" continued:
- Aaron struck the Nile River with his staff and the water turned to blood; the magicians turned some water to blood (Exod. 7:20-22).
- Aaron raised his staff over all the rivers, canals, and ponds in Egypt and brought a plague of frogs; the magicians caused some frogs to appear (Exod. 8:6-7).
- Aaron raised his staff and struck the ground and this brought swarms of gnats throughout the land of Egypt. However, this time when Pharaoh's magicians attempted to imitate what God had done, they failed (Exod. 8:16-18).

# "Where there is an original of value, there is often a flawed imitation; only God is The Original."

"This is the finger of God" (Exod. 8:19), the magicians told Pharaoh. After that, God brought plagues of flies, death to livestock, boils, hail, locusts, and darkness (Exod. 8:20-10:23). Never again does it say that Pharaoh's magicians even tried to imitate the plagues that God brought to the land of Egypt. Indeed, by the time the Israelites left Egypt it was clear to all that God delivered them with His power and might. Egyptians and Israelites alike acknowledged that God is "The Original."

**Where there is an original of value, there is often a flawed imitation; only God is "The Original."**

Satan watched God perform marvelous works countless times, but Satan's imitation of "The Original" is flawed and ineffective. Just as Pharaoh's magicians imitated God, people today do the same thing. An author may slip a Bible verse or two into an otherwise worldly book or podcast or blog as an imitation of "The Original;" a speaker may skillfully scatter godly phrases in a speech to camouflage an otherwise sinful message. Cults spring up that have some of the truth of God's Word, but instead are imitations. We must diligently use our spiritual radar to determine the difference.

Even our imitation of "The Original" is just that. Though doing our best to imitate Him is certainly scriptural (Eph. 5:1), only God is "The Original." He is the "Alpha and Omega ... the beginning and the end" (Rev. 22:13). He is omniscient, omnipresent, and omnipotent. He is perfect in all of His ways. Beware of imitations; only "The Original" deserves our worship, praise, and loyalty. So, as we imitate Christ, be certain to point others to "The Original," the only One with the unique ability to transform their lives.

# 8

## WEEK EIGHT
### *NEIGHBOR*

EXODUS 16-17

EXODUS 18-19

EXODUS 20-21

EXODUS 22-23

EXODUS 24-25

## MEMORY VERSE

"BE KIND AND COMPASSIONATE TO ONE ANOTHER,
FORGIVING EACH OTHER, JUST AS IN CHRIST GOD
FORGAVE YOU."

**EPHESIANS 4:32**

# LOVING YOUR NEIGHBOR, LOVING YOURSELF

**BY KRISTEN WILLIAMSON**

I can't tell you the number of difficult people I have met in my life. What I've learned in recent years though is that (usually) those people aren't actually the difficult ones, I am.

I would confidently walk around saying, "God creates everyone perfectly" and "we should love our neighbor," but what I was living out is: my neighbors need fixing and I'm the only perfectly made human here. Sure, I make mistakes, but surely, I can't be difficult. It sounds harsh, and it is.

You know who else likely felt this way? The Israelites wandering through the wilderness with Moses. In Exodus 16,  the Israelites are in their second month of wandering through the wilderness. They have faced the harshest realities through this journey, to the point they even consider going back to oppression and slavery to be better than this. They surely couldn't be difficult or flawed. But you know who was making life pretty difficult for them? Moses.

Even though God appointed Moses to lead them through the wilderness and confirmed this truth time after time, they were too disconnected from God to fully understand the situation. They're grumblings weren't being heard by Moses, they were being heard and felt by God. Moses stopped them to ask, "why do you quarrel with me? Why do you test the Lord?" (Exod. 17:1). They even frustrated themselves to the point of wishing they would simply die before following Moses any longer (Exod. 16:3).

*Ouch.*

What a way to feel about a leader appointed by God. That death would be better than following him. Again, sounds harsh, right? It is.

So how do we soften our hearts? *Obedience and prayer.*

"So let us continually be seeking opportunities to obey God's will so that we can be a light in this world."

Moses isn't without difficulties himself, none of us are. He's killed, run away, made excuses for what God called him to do, disobeyed God, and so much more. However, Moses continually turned to prayer and actively tried to obey what God commanded of him. He had his moments of doubt, but for the majority of his life, he completely trusted and obeyed God. Moses actively sought God, prayed that God would use him and guide him, and acted as a messenger of God in the first five books of the Bible.

**So let us continually be seeking opportunities to obey God's will so that we can be a light in this world.** It's a humbling experience, just like wandering in the wilderness for forty years, to be obedient even when it isn't easy.

But it becomes slightly easier when we remember why we are being obedient. Why we continue to press on through the hard things: because God is good. Because God's perfect will is better than anything we might have in mind for our lives. So we trust Him and we pray. We pray that God would show His will to us and give us the hearts to be used by Him. To soften our hearts so that we can shine His light to those around us.

These two things won't make it so that we aren't difficult in the eyes of others and our neighbors will never again be difficult to us. But it does mean that we can delight in His works being done in us and in the hearts of others.

This week I challenge you to find the difficult or challenging people in your life and pursue them. Pray for them, pray with them, get into God's word with them. And don't forget to pray over your heart too.

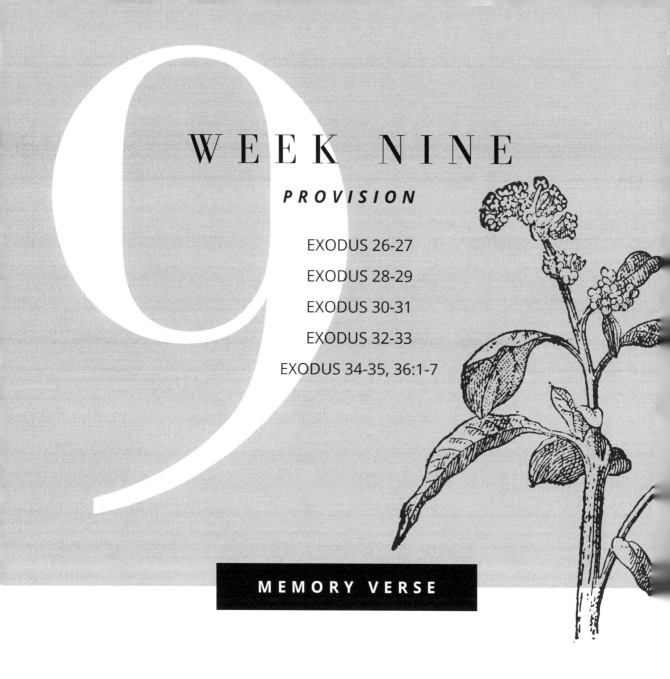

# 9

## WEEK NINE

### *PROVISION*

EXODUS 26-27

EXODUS 28-29

EXODUS 30-31

EXODUS 32-33

EXODUS 34-35, 36:1-7

**MEMORY VERSE**

"FOR WE ARE GOD'S HANDIWORK, CREATED IN CHRIST JESUS TO DO GOOD WORKS, WHICH GOD PREPARED IN ADVANCE FOR US TO DO."

EPHESIANS 2:10

# SKILL AND THE WILL

**BY TIERNEY NASHLEANAS**

As I held my fresh, blue-eyed boy in my arms for the first time, I felt a herd of emotions. I felt happiness that he was here, disbelief at how precious he was, relief that labor and delivery was over, excitement to see him grow but also paralyzing fear for the task set before me and pressure to "do it right."

My son, perfectly knitted together, was given to me by God to care for, love and raise up. Yet, in an overwhelming wave of anxiety, 6lbs 4oz felt heavy. The details as to how my husband and I would raise this precious one felt impossible.

In Exodus, the LORD met with Moses on the mountain and gave him plans for the construction of the tabernacle, a place where he would meet with his people. These plans included exact specifications for the size, artistic detail, materials and functional use. Beautiful materials would be used, including precious metals, acacia wood and fine linen of vivid colors.

How would this beautiful tabernacle be raised and where would the materials come from?

God called Bezalel by name (Exod. 31:2 ESV) and "filled him with the Spirit of God, with wisdom, with understanding, with knowledge and with all kinds of skills to make artistic designs..." (Exod. 31: 3-4 NIV) to make the tabernacle. In the days of Egypt, when it was all Bezalel could do to put one foot in front of the other, God was forging in him the skills he needed for the day the Spirit of God would empower him to raise the tabernacle for His glory and the welfare of Israel.

In chapter 35, God commanded His people to bring supplies (that they took with them when they left Egypt), with generous hearts, and skills, with willing hands, to contribute to the construction of the tabernacle. God used their exodus from Egypt to provide for the materials used in the creation of an even greater blessing.

**God is faithful to provide the skill and the will to complete the work He sets before us.**

As I think about all the joyful, beautiful, scary, hard and hopeful times both you and I face as moms, I am encouraged by the good news that God does the same for us. If God was faithful to provide for the Israelites in the raising of the tabernacle, how much more will He provide for you in the raising of your children? You have been called by name to belong to God through Jesus, and he has given you his Spirit to empower you with the skill and the will to complete the work of loving, caring for and investing in those around you.

Sister, because of Christ, you have everything you need to fulfill your God-given calling. Remember, he has given you his Spirit, he is with you, and he is using the trials of your daily life to forge in you everything you need for your sacred calling.

"God is faithful to provide the skill and the will to complete the work He sets before us."

# 10

## WEEK TEN

### OBEDIENCE

EXODUS 40, LEVITICUS 19

LEVITICUS 20-21

LEVITICUS 23, 26

NUMBERS 9, 10:11-13, 10:29-36

NUMBERS 11, 13

**MEMORY VERSE**

"OBEY ME, AND I WILL BE YOUR GOD AND YOU WILL
BE MY PEOPLE. WALK IN OBEDIENCE TO ALL I
COMMAND YOU, THAT IT MAY GO WELL WITH YOU."

JEREMIAH 7:23

# CALLED TO CARRY HIS PRESENCE

**BY NANCY EHLINGER**

When our kids were little, my husband and I attended a seminar on how to raise Godly children. One of the games we learned to play to instill obedience was to "come when I call your name." It went like this. Your child stands behind an imaginary line and they wait until you call their name before they come running. "Wait. Wait. No, wait. Moses, come." As they learn, you continually increase the waiting time. They learn to come when you call. This is an important skill we can all use even as adults.

As I studied this week's scripture, it felt overwhelming. I haven't always been good at following a lot of rules. Although I like structure and knowing the parameters I am to work within, I often find myself choosing my own path instead of God's. Obedience isn't always my strong suit, but "Moses did everything just as the Lord commanded him" (Exod. 40:16).

Reading through Exodus, Leviticus, and Numbers, the list of laws probably feels restrictive, even archaic. To our 21st-century lives, they may even appear completely unnecessary. Leviticus 19:19 ends by telling us not to wear clothing woven of two kinds of material preceded by those rules we should still follow: "Do not seek revenge or bear a grudge against anyone among your people but love your neighbor as yourself. I am the Lord" (Lev. 19:18).

During the 40 years spent traveling from Egypt to Canaan, from slavery to freedom, God was teaching them obedience. Come when I call your name. God's plan was to teach a new generation what was holy and how to treat the things of God as holy. As God gave Moses specific instructions to set up the tabernacle which carried the presence of God, his sons were watching him. The next generation was learning to be obedient, to follow God.

As we travel with the Israelites through the desert, we can see how God continued calling them with tangible signs: "In all the travels of the Israelites, whenever the cloud lifted from above the tabernacle, they would set out; but if the cloud did not lift, they did not set out until the day it lifted" (Exod. 40:36).

"Instead of living in a box, God's presence lives in us."

As God continually moved before them, He was calling them out of the darkness of the slavery of Egypt, preparing his people for the Messiah.

The Messiah says the greatest commandment is to "'Love the Lord your God with all your heart and with all your soul and with all your mind.' This is the first and greatest commandment. And the second is like it: 'Love your neighbor as yourself. All the Law and the Prophets hang on these two commandments'" (Matt. 22:39).

Jesus didn't come to abolish the law. He came to fulfill it. God knew we could never keep all 613 laws on our own. When we love God with our mind, soul, and strength, His love will overflow as we learn to love our neighbors.

As Jesus hung on the cross, He opened the door for us to become a temple of the living God. **Instead of living in a box, God's presence lives in us.** His presence calls us to obedience.

Although obedience looks different for each of us, our love of God and His love of us will spill over into the world around us. What is God calling you to do? Maybe it's having coffee with a friend or meeting some other moms at the park.

You won't leave Egypt alone. *He is with you.*

WEEK TEN TAKEAWAY

# HOW TO STUDY THE BIBLE
## (when you're not an expert)

**1** Remember the purpose of God's Word. The Bible is God's story. It teaches us His character and His ways. God's Word gives us a firm foundation of truth to build our lives on, and teaches us Kingdom ways of living. It is not a book of requirements to which we must fulfill in order to satisfy God. Rather, the Bible reveals our absolute inability to measure up, deepening our dependence on Christ.

**2** Remember the goal of study is growth (not just "checking a box" or accumulating information). "Study" insinuates more than reading. When we study the Bible, the intention is to understand what God is teaching us about Himself, so that we may apply it to our lives, and grow in our relationship with Him. For help understanding and applying God's Word to your everyday life, utilize the R.O.O.T. journaling method (guides found on pages 9, 100, 136, and 169).

**3** Depend on the Holy Spirit. We need God's help to understand His Word. This is why the Psalmist, David, prayed over and over phrases such as— *"Give me understanding..."* (Ps. 119:73), *"Open my eyes..."* (Ps. 119:18), and *"Cause me to understand..."* (Ps. 119:27) The Holy Spirit is called the "Helper" (John 14:16). Jesus said that the Holy Spirit guides us "into all the truth" (Jn. 16:13). He convicts us of sin (John 16:8), comforts us (John 14:16), teaches us (John 14:26), and glorifies Jesus (John 16:14). When approaching God's Word, take a moment to pause and admit your need for the Holy Spirit, and invoke His help.

**4** Don't get lost in the details (zoom out to see the big picture). It's fun to do the occasional deep dive on a Greek or Hebrew Word, or a long study on a particular topic or passage. But don't forget the Bible is not a collection of isolated verses and stories, but rather each one is deeply interconnected. When reading a passage, ask the question, "How does this fit into the bigger picture of the Gospel?"

**5** Intentionality > time. Fifteen minutes of focused study can be just as productive as an hour of distracted study. It's intention that matters most. Show up ready to receive the "daily bread" God has for you. Choose a time of day when your mind is alert. Prepare your heart through prayer (see tip #3), and put your phone on airplane mode. For more help on making the most of your minutes, see our Quiet Time Guide on page 30.

**Utilize reliable resources.** Most of us will never attend Bible school, but we can look to the experts for help understanding the context, cultural elements, and implications of a passage. Be weary of random internet searches, and seek out reliable resources. Check out our team's favorites at www.rootedmoms.com/study.

**Remember it's not about you**. To rightly study God's Word, we must understand that *every* story points to Jesus. When we start making the Bible about us we worship ourselves and our own ability instead of the One it was written to glorify so that we may treasure Him more deeply.

We are not the hero; only He is. How do we put this study filter into practice? For example, most of us read the story of Esther and would takeaway an idea such as, "I need to be more bold like Esther and willing to risk my life for others." While that's a good and noble goal, it undermines the truth that "Jesus is the true and better Esther who didn't just risk leaving an earthly palace but lost the ultimate and heavenly one, who didn't just risk his life, but gave his life to save his people."*

**Look for the Gospel (good news).** Your study should never end in guilt, shame or feeling laden with a heavy burden. Reading God's Word should increase our joy, as we meditate on all He has done, is doing, and will do for us. In Christ, the news is always good, friends. When we read a passage that reminds us of our past sins, we can remember they are covered under the blood of Jesus. When we read a command that feels impossible to live up to, we can remember we are empowered by the Holy Spirit. When we feel convicted, we can confess and repent knowing there is no condemnation for those who are in Christ Jesus. *Don't stop until you reach the joy!*

**Don't get stuck in a rut.** Be flexible and creative! Change up your study routine often. Studying your Bible should be something you look forward to, not a chore to get done. Utilize different study methods and resources to keep your mind engaged. Try a different location or time of day. Incorporate elements that help you commune with God such as worship, prayer, and movement. Bible study doesn't have to be dull and redundant!

**Process what you are learning**. Write out your observations and takeaways in a journal. Meet with a friend over coffee to share what God is speaking to you. Join a Bible study group where you can discuss each week's reading. For more on why community is important to growing in God's Word, see our "Better Together" resource on page 198.

*Keller, Timothy. *Preaching: Communicating Faith in an Age of Skepticism.* Penguin Books, 2015

# WEEK ELEVEN

## *FAITH*

NUMBERS 14, 20

NUMBERS 22, 23

NUMBERS 24, 27:12-23, 33:50-56

DEUTERONOMY 1, 4

DEUTERONOMY 6, 8

### MEMORY VERSE

"HE IS THE ROCK, HIS WORKS ARE PERFECT, AND ALL HIS WAYS ARE JUST. A FAITHFUL GOD WHO DOES NO WRONG, UPRIGHT AND JUST IS HE."

**DEUTERONOMY 32:4**

# REMEMBER GOD'S GOODNESS

**BY AUDRA POWERS**

My husband and I stood at an impasse. His job security was at stake; his livelihood on the line. Never in a million years did we think his very secure job would be threatened. We fasted, prayed, and pleaded with God to make a way. Our pastor counseled us to remember God's past faithfulness in our lives as we faced an uncertain future.

Remembering God helped us walk the uncertain road with very certain faith. The more we recounted divine moments, milestones, and miracles, the more our trust, love, and obedience grew. Our pleas turned into praise. Remembering the past helped us move forward in faith, even when we couldn't see the future.

In Deuteronomy 8, Moses is commanding the Israelites to remember what God has done. Why? Remembrance leads to obedience. Remembering God's past faithfulness would fuel their future obedience. Moses urged the people to remember their slavery in Egypt, how God delivered them, and why they must not elevate idols over the one true living God lest they perish (Deut. 8:18-20).

Moses lists a multitude of manifestations of God from miracles to manna. He warns them to keep their hearts humble so they don't turn away from the Lord their God when life is good. Moses warns against complacency which can lead to worshiping idols over the one true living God. If they forget God's faithfulness, they will be tempted to turn to other gods instead of obeying the Lord their God.

It's wise for us to consider Moses' warnings and commands to the people of Israel. Although we are not slaves in Egypt, we were slaves to sin before God freed us. Our modern day problems may be different, but our source is still the same: the one true living God. Yet our human hearts can be quick to place our hope in a job instead of God.

Even when life is downright hard, we can walk by faith in obedience to God when we remember who sustains us in this life, nothing else.

**Remembrance leads to obedience.** Not only is our faith strengthened, but our love for God grows deeper when we focus on how God weaves our story, provides for our families, and makes manna rain down in the desert seasons.

In all our remembering, we also remember we didn't earn the job, God gave it to us. We can allow the times of uncertainty to remind us we achieve nothing in our own strength, but only by God's grace, "Beware lest you say in your heart, 'My power and the might of my hand have gotten me this wealth.' You shall remember the Lord for it is he who gives you power to get wealth, that he may confirm his covenant he swore to your fathers, as it is this day" (Deut. 8:17-18 ESV).

If God gave you this job, He will give you another one. If God gave you a home, He will provide a new place to live. If God gave you a family, He will sustain you in raising up your children. If he brought you to it, He will bring you through it. He is your ultimate source. And He is always faithful.

How can you practice Moses' command in your modern day life? Remember, write, and rejoice. Remember specific moments of God's faithfulness, write them down, and then rejoice over them with prayers of thanksgiving and songs of praise.

"Remembrance leads to obedience."

# WEEK TWELVE

## *REMEMBER*

DEUTERONOMY 9, 11

DEUTERONOMY 29, 30

DEUTERONOMY 31, 34

JOSHUA 1-2

JOSHUA 3-4

**MEMORY VERSE**

"IN THE NIGHT, LORD, I REMEMBER YOUR NAME,
THAT I MAY KEEP YOUR LAW."

**PSALM 119:55**

# CHOOSING TO REMEMBER

**BY WENDY GERDES**

"Tell me about a time when you KNEW God answered a prayer you prayed," I said to the class of bright-eyed 4th grade girls seated in front of me. One sweet girl raised her hand exuberantly and I quickly called on her.

With a big smile on her face, she said, "Last week, my mom realized I had outgrown all of my clothes and we didn't have any money for new ones. We prayed together and the next day, someone gave us two full bags of clothes! They fit both me and my sister perfectly!" A story of God's faithfulness displayed. A monument in her little mind that the big God cares for her. If she ever feels uncared for, that story will be a bearer of truth to her heart. God cares. He's good. He can be trusted. The day bags of needed clothes showed up, a little root grew that would anchor her. This story, when shared and remembered, ignites faith and reminds us of who God is.

In Deuteronomy 11, remembering what God had done is directly linked to obedience. We will not obey a God we do not think we can trust. The chapter begins in verse 1 with Moses declaring that the Israelites are to love God and keep his statutes, ordinances, and commands. Next he reminds them in verses 2-7 that although they had seen firsthand God's discipline, deliverance from Egypt, provision in the wilderness, and holiness displayed, their children had not. Their children needed the stories to build their faith in the holy and good God until they had stories of their own.

In verse 19, Moses makes it clear they were to teach their children God's commands daily and in ordinary moments: sitting at home, walking, at bedtime and in the morning. Their stories told to the next generation would pass on knowledge of God's greatness, goodness and holiness. The commands were what they needed to do, but the stories revealed who they were obeying. Without remembering, their children would not know God's heart or holiness and laws would become arbitrary and disconnected from a good God. Obedience requires trust in a good God.

"Stories preserved become a foundation for faith and obedience to be built upon."

Faith travels through stories. Sharing our faith with the next generation not only means sharing beloved truths and Bible stories but also new stories. The stories where God shows up in our ordinary lives teach our children the faithfulness of God and encourage them to follow Him in their ordinary lives. Stories build faith and obedience rests on faith.

It is our forgetfulness of God that causes us to lose faith and eventually disobey. When we don't remember who God is or what He has done, we begin to put more faith in ourselves or things around us than in Him. Tragically, eventually the Israelites forgot and turned from God. Forgetting is easy when remembering isn't intentionally woven into the fabric of our lives. **Stories preserved become a foundation for faith and obedience to be built upon.**

As parents of God's created, we are tasked with the responsibility of teaching Him to them in normal, everyday life. We are storytellers. They learn about Him in Bible stories and teaching His ways, but also through personal stories we tell. Not only do stories help our children to remember, but they help us and others who hear.

We easily forget, but we can choose to remember. Let's be ones who remember and tell the stories of God's kind generosity and faithfulness to us.

# WEEK THIRTEEN

## *TRUST*

JOSHUA 5-6

JOSHUA 7-8

JOSHUA 9-10

JOSHUA 23-24

JUDGES 2-3

**MEMORY VERSE**

"TRUST IN THE LORD WITH ALL YOUR HEART AND
LEAN NOT ON YOUR OWN UNDERSTANDING; IN ALL
YOUR WAYS SUBMIT TO HIM, AND HE WILL MAKE
YOUR PATHS STRAIGHT."

**PROVERBS 3:5-6**

# A FULLY SURRENDERED LIFE

**BY SARETTA WELLS**

I am prone to want to control situations and to try to figure things out on my own. From an early age, I was able to discern things well, and I would seek to prevent problems or get my way. I thought I was managing my life pretty well, but I was anxious. My brain wouldn't stop. I worried about what people thought of things I did. There were problems (real or imaginary) at every turn. I'd have entire conversations in my head, pretending I knew what others were thinking or what might come. It was exhausting, but on the outside I looked like I had it all together and lived what others would view as a successful life. I was deceived.

After seventeen years of trying my absolute best to follow Jesus, I met the Holy Spirit in a life-altering way, and my entire world changed. I quickly learned that He had work for me every single day, moment by moment. Simple obedience became my entire life. I realized that I had been stifling His voice for years. As COVID-19 hit, I would wait on His command to do even simple things such as make online grocery orders, and while many weren't getting large portions of their orders, mine was always full. I was both shocked and hooked...my anxiety completely gone because of full faith in His ways. While, in the past, I thought I could plan certain things easily, I now realized the value and subsequent fruit brought about from seeking His input.

When I read that Israel sampled Gibeon's provisions and didn't inquire of the Lord (Jos. 9:14), my heart broke because I know that is how I lived for so long. They leaned on their understanding of what they were hearing and seeing instead on the complete knowledge of the Father. They saw worn clothing and moldy bread and made the decision themselves that these people were truly from far away (Jos. 9:12-13). The Lord could have revealed who the Gibeonites were if He had been consulted, and this story would have ended quite differently.

The Gibeonites would have been destroyed completely. Instead, the Israelites were deceived and bound to them (Jos. 9:15). This treaty with a people that would've been destroyed ultimately led to a famine in the time of David due to Saul's later destruction of the Gibeonites (2 Sam. 21:1).

I wonder if they ever wondered what might have been if they had sought the Lord instead of trusting in man. Did they wish they could have gone back and done it differently? In our lives, our confidence comes when we seek Him in all things and move according to His will. **There is no greater life than living fully surrendered to Jesus.**

Does the idea that He wants access to everything (our finances, our parenting, our marriage, and even how we spend our time) sound scary? I would have said 'yes' to that question for years, but let me encourage you: He is a good Father. He is not bound by time or space, and his knowledge is not limited. He is trustworthy, and He is truly found by those who seek Him with all their hearts.

As we continue to read His great book, we will come to know His heart for us more and more, and our faith and trust will grow. While that journey will likely last a lifetime, let's start living in that trust now. If we think we know how to handle a situation, let's check with Him anyway. When what we see leads us to only one conclusion, let's ask Him for His input anyway. He is the only one that truly sees all aspects. Trust Him with me, and let's live the full life that Jesus says He came to give!

# WEEK FOURTEEN

## IDENTITY

JUDGES 4, 6

JUDGES 7, 13

JUDGES 14-16

RUTH 1-2

RUTH 3-4

**MEMORY VERSE**

"BUT YOU ARE A CHOSEN PEOPLE, A ROYAL PRIESTHOOD, A HOLY NATION, GOD'S SPECIAL POSSESSION, THAT YOU MAY DECLARE THE PRAISES OF HIM WHO CALLED YOU OUT OF DARKNESS INTO HIS WONDERFUL LIGHT."

**1 PETER 2:9**

# NOT WHAT I SEE IN THE MIRROR

**BY HEATHER KENNY**

Have your life circumstances ever pushed you into hiding? Like many women, I struggle with mental illness. The first time it reared its ugly head, I was full of shame and embarrassment, and I found myself pulling away from people and life. I was hiding again a year ago under different circumstances. A horrifically tragic incident happened next to our property when a young teen was accidentally killed by a police officer. We were suddenly under intense scrutiny and in the public eye, making national news, simply for being nearby property owners. Hiding often feels safer than facing scary circumstances.

As I write this, Russia has been attacking Ukraine for two full months. Myriad people have been pushed into hiding in an attempt to save what is left of their lives. People are scared, confused, and desperate for relief.

We find Israel facing a similar situation in Judges chapter six. Neighboring Midianites have been oppressing the Israelite people for seven years. Things have become desperate. Families have fled their homes for the relative safety of mountain caves and dens. Every year, as soon as crops have been planted, Midianite armies invade with the intention of destroying every bit of sustenance being grown. The Israelites have been reduced to almost nothing - devoid of hope, full of fear and despair.

In the midst of this, we meet Gideon, a young Israelite who is threshing wheat at the bottom of a winepress. What a strange sight this would have been! Threshing wheat is one of the most labor-intensive processes outside of the modern machinery used today. The ultimate goal is to separate the edible wheat kernels from the straw and chaff. Traditionally, this was done in wide-open spaces, probably on a day when a gentle breeze was blowing, allowing the heavier wheat kernels to fall to the ground as the chaff blew away.

Imagine doing that in an enclosed area.

> "God has this incredible way of speaking our identities into our lives before we can see that identity in the mirror."

Gideon is right there, in the middle of his mess, hiding from his circumstances, when an angel of the Lord appears and addresses him, "The Lord is with you, mighty warrior" (Judg. 6:12b).

Whoa. Read that again: "The Lord is with you, mighty warrior."

Do you think Gideon felt like a mighty warrior as he cowered in the shadows, afraid for his life? I doubt it. **God has this incredible way of speaking our identities into our lives before we can see that identity in the mirror.**

When I look in the mirror, I see a woman who struggles with mental illness, doesn't pray "enough", hasn't been to a physical church in three years, and who picks fights with her husband. But God tells me that's not who I am in Him. He calls me a daughter of the King, beloved, forgiven, and perfect in His sight.

*Whew.*

It doesn't really matter what you are hiding from today. What matters is that you remind yourself who God says you are. You are a daughter of the King, forgiven, worthy, loved, a masterpiece, chosen, significant, and gifted. Place intentional reminders around you so that you can see the truth when you feel like hiding. Make a list of your true identity on a post-it note and put it on your mirror or steering wheel, make a wallpaper for your phone, or set a reminder on your phone at a certain time every day. Step out of hiding, my friend, and embrace who God says you are.

# WEEK FIFTEEN

## *RELEASE*

1 SAMUEL 1-2

1 SAMUEL 3, 8

1 SAMUEL 9-10, 11:12-15

1 SAMUEL 12-13

1 SAMUEL 14-15

**MEMORY VERSE**

"THE LORD IS MY STRENGTH AND MY SHIELD; MY HEART TRUSTS IN HIM AND HE HELPS ME. MY HEART LEAPS FOR JOY, AND WITH MY SONG I PRAISE HIM."

**PSALM 28:7**

# UNCLENCHING OUR GRIP

**BY RENEE ROBINSON**

Sitting around the table swapping stories, my friend took us down memory lane to when her adult son was a young boy. Thinking he went back to sleep after recovering from illness, they found him in a coma. Rushing him to the hospital, they prayed fervently. When the doctor visited the family the first time, he informed them that her son had diabetes and had fallen into a diabetic coma. Based on the amount of time and the severity, his chances of survival were very slim. The doctor's words came with a devastating message of a preparation for the greatest loss the family could imagine.

My friend lowered herself to her knees and bowed her head, "Lord, I have treasured every moment of the nine years you allowed me to spend with my precious son. But he is also your son, so I am surrendering him back to You."

Within moments of praying, she stretched her body across the row of blue vinyl hospital chairs. Closing her eyes, she drifted into what she describes as the deepest sleep she ever remembered experiencing, the Lord's peace her blanket. When she awakened, the doctor shared the miraculous news that her son was alive and well.

She surrendered the greatest blessing of her life to the Lord and trusted Him whether she faced a loss or a miracle.

In Samuel chapter 1, Hannah longed for a baby, yet as time passed she remained childless. Hannah took her deep wounds and poured out her bitter tears to the Lord promising Him that if He gave her a son, she vowed to give him back to the Lord all the days of his life (1 Sam. 1:11).

The Lord remembered Hannah and blessed her with the son she desperately longed for. Hannah remembered her vow, "and she said to him, 'Pardon me, my lord. As surely as you live, I am the woman who stood here beside you praying to the Lord. I prayed for this child, and the Lord has granted me what I asked of him. So now I give him to the Lord. For his whole life he will be given over to the Lord'" (1 Sam. 1: 26-28).

Hannah waited for the blessing of a son, and when she received it, she opened her hand and released him back to the Lord. Our children are God's children first. He's entrusted them to our care, but He loves them more than we do. It's human nature for us to parent with clenched fists, fretting, and desiring to control what often is uncontrollable. We long for the very best for our children. So does God.
We can surrender our children to the Lord and trust Him no matter what happens out of our control. Children are a blessing and a reward, and we often desire to hold tight to these blessed rewards.

**Surrender requires deep trust, but the reward is unshakeable peace.**

What deep desires or longings are you holding with clenched fists? Open your hands and surrender them to the Lord. As you open your hands, reach toward God and grasp His hand as you give those deepest cares and concerns back to Him. You can trust Him with anything you place in His loving hands.

"Surrender requires deep trust, but the reward is unshakeable peace."

# WHEN "QUIET" TIME ISN'T QUIET

## meeting Jesus in the mess of motherhood

"I love to have my quiet time alone, in the mornings before anyone else in the house wakes up. However, if my morning time is interrupted I try to let whichever child it is take part. My kids are 4 and 6, and usually can sit still with me for a little while. I will read the passages out loud to them and answer any questions they may have or listen to their takeaway. If they are not having it, I will put my Bible aside and start the day while listening to worship music. It puts everyone in a better mood, including myself and I give myself grace for things that are not going as planned. When that happens I will take my Bible to read during carline or dive into a commentary about that particular week's reading. Sometimes I will read at night. **God has taught me to not become frustrated, and to enjoy the now and be present for my most precious disciples.**" —Brenna K.

"I have a 6 year old and a 3 year old. My 3 year old wakes up before the sun comes up so waking up early for quiet time doesn't work for my schedule right now. My quiet time happens right now either in the carline or after I put the kids down for bed. I've learned that God doesn't care *when* you spend time with Him just as long as you *do* spend time with Him. **A great tool I'm utilizing right now when I do my quiet time in the car line is the Youversion app.** I'll highlight passages and add my notes in the app then later transfer them to my notebook. That way I never have the excuse I don't have my Bible or my notebook." —Tara M.

"I have two littles under the age of 5, so no matter what I plan, my quiet time looks a little different each day. My older one (4), knows that first thing in the morning is when Mommy likes to read her Bible and pray. **She just likes to be near me and doing what I am doing, so recently I got her her own journal and "fancy" pens.** She loves sitting next to me and writing in her journal as I write in mine. I gave her an old Bible to flip through the pages while I read my mine. If my 19-month-old wakes up early, then it typically means that I will be pushing my quiet time until later. On those days my morning "quiet" time looks like listening to commentary in the car on the way to and from preschool, then sitting down during nap time for my reading and journaling." —Jessica P.

"Even with a routine, life with little ones is unpredictable. With two little boys and one on the way, ideal quiet times are few and far between.  My ideal quiet time is in the morning before my boys awake, before I have to do anything for anyone including myself, but it doesn't always happen anymore. Frequent sleepless nights mean having a consistent quiet time in the morning is not always feasible. So, with each new day, I grant myself grace and find time in my day to connect with my God. Sometimes those ideal quiet times happen, but when they don't, find a nugget of time during your day (nap time, play time, after bedtime or even begin anew the next day) to spend with God. **See what your God can do when you connect with Him in those nuggets of time throughout your day.**" —Brooke P.

"My kids are 13, 12, and 8. Most days I try to wake up before they do, but some days that doesn't happen. On those mornings I often study with the background noise of YouTube, with frequent interruptions for homework help, etc. **In those frustrating moments, I remind myself that God is not unaware of my season of life.** A patient response to my children's needs communicates they are important to both me and Him. Also, I remember 'monkey see, monkey do.' By taking time to spend with Jesus (even when it's not convenient), I am modeling what it looks like to walk with God in real life. Last week I went to check in on my daughter and she was reading and taking notes from her Bible. More is caught than taught. Let your kids 'catch you' pursuing Jesus!" —Katie G.

"My quiet time looks different everyday because with kids everyday *is* different. Recently I woke up early for my quiet time and my daughters (6 and 2) came in and crashed. They really needed some cuddles. I don't think God would want me to push them away in order to concentrate because motherhood is obviously something He has called me into! **God has taught me to roll with the punches and has reminded me, it's not a checklist—** *it is a relationship.* When you're in a relationship with the Lord, He provides an abundance of grace for these moments. Our job is to receive it. When my kids crash my quiet time, I extend that grace to them and invite them up on the couch. If we aim for perfection, we wind up feeling burned out. Sometimes spending time with Him looks like two pages of notes, and sometimes that looks like a five minute commentary and praying throughout your day." —Taylor W.

"I have a 5 year old and a 19 month old, so quiet time can look a little different when each girl is up in my business. **When it comes to my 5 year old, I  have her sit at the table with me and while I do my quiet time, I give her something to work on also (think art activity or letter/number tracing).** This makes her feel like she is doing something big like mama and then we have story time about what I've read. With my 19-month-old, I revert to something much more simple and that is listening to commentary in the car or while we are doing things around the house. This ensures I am getting in the Word and getting a deeper understanding, then if I have more time later, it is easier to take down notes while I read through." —Brittany M.

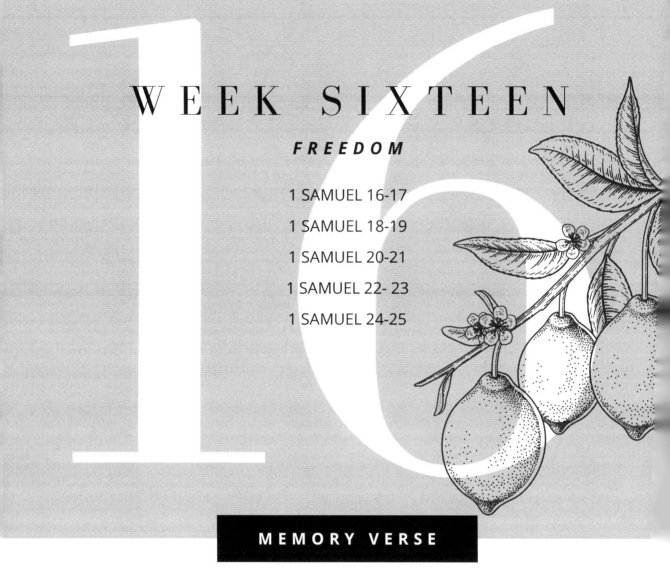

# WEEK SIXTEEN

### FREEDOM

1 SAMUEL 16-17

1 SAMUEL 18-19

1 SAMUEL 20-21

1 SAMUEL 22- 23

1 SAMUEL 24-25

## MEMORY VERSE

"BUT WHO CAN DISCERN THEIR OWN ERRORS? FORGIVE
MY HIDDEN FAULTS. KEEP YOUR SERVANT ALSO FROM
WILLFUL SINS; MAY THEY NOT RULE OVER ME."

**PSALM 19:12-13A**

# BROKEN CHAINS

**BY BRENNA KURZ**

When I was younger, I was passionate—to a *fault.*

Quick to anger and slow to back down, even when I was wrong. I thought having the last word meant I won the fight. Have you ever felt this way?

I was well into my marriage when I realized the seriousness of the problem at hand. Every time we argued, I would not be the one to say 'sorry.' My stubbornness would go into defense mode and I would be sure to point out all of his errors while I kept the sin, that I didn't know I had, hidden.

In 1 Samuel 24, David shows compassion and spares the life of Saul after he had been hunting him for twenty years. I am sure David surprised himself with his response, but he understood that God was in control and that His will would be done in His perfect timing.

David told his men that encouraged him to lash out against Saul, "The Lord forbid that I should do such a thing to my master, the Lord's anointed, or lay a hand on him; for he is the anointed of the Lord" (1 Sam. 24:6).

David had his own struggles throughout his life, just like we do, but he knew that his retribution would not honor God. His faithfulness to honor God over his feelings in the moment was more important. Feelings tell lies, but God is faithful to keep His promises to us.

That is when I understood that I was more like Saul than I would like to admit. Years later, after the realization that my way was not working, I finally turned to the Lord for answers. He revealed to me my hidden faults. It took everything in me to surrender the sin at hand: pride. God gently exposed my sin and softened my heart, but this realization hurt! I then understood that the anger, bitterness and pain I experienced and caused others was not of the Lord. I used to see having the last word as a victory medal, now I see they were chains.

# "A surrendered heart breaks the chains that keep us trapped in sin."

After I repented, God washed over my pain with His peace. The weight of those shackles needed to be broken so I could live the life He intended for me.

Shortly after I surrendered, God put it on my husband's heart to share a sin he'd been keeping in the dark. I knew I had to step out of my own way and that was when I noticed my response was not my own but God's.

**A surrendered heart breaks the chains that keep us trapped in sin.**

When we are so consumed with pride, jealousy and our own emotions, it is quite difficult to see when we are the problem. Satan wants to make us comfortable in the dark. Hiding our sin and masking it with our pride makes his job that much easier.

But friend, let's remember to not be controlled by our own selfishness and look at the situation from the perspective of our trustworthy God. When things get hard and relationships get sticky, remember the love God wants to extend. He exposes our sin because He is light and He disciplines the ones He loves (Pr. 3:11-12). Let's humble ourselves and yield to the Lord, keeping our eyes fixed on our loving Father.

Surrender to Him today and watch as the chains are broken. Let Him have the last word because He is worthy!

# 17

## WEEK SEVENTEEN

### PRESENCE

1 SAMUEL 26, 28:3-25

1 SAMUEL 30-31

2 SAMUEL 1-3:1

2 SAMUEL 5-6

2 SAMUEL 7, 9

## MEMORY VERSE

"BECAUSE YOUR LOVE IS BETTER THAN LIFE,
MY LIPS WILL GLORIFY YOU. I WILL PRAISE
YOU AS LONG AS I LIVE, AND IN YOUR NAME I
WILL LIFT UP MY HANDS."

**PSALM 63: 3-4**

# HIS PRESENCE IS THE PRIZE

**BY TIERNEY NASHLEANAS**

Hope rested in my heart as my husband and I looked out over the bouncing waves to the sun as it began its evening dive into the ocean. Would we see it? A crowd was beginning to gather along the shoreline; the air was charged with a sense of expectancy. The horizon changed from lively shades of yellow to sleepy shades of orange and the gentle hum from the people on the beach faded into silence. As the sun closed its eyelid to sleep, the beautifully vivid glow of neon green light hovered over the water before it, too, went to sleep. There was dancing, cheering, clapping and much unashamed rejoicing in response to seeing the sunset's green flash. One man even yelled, "Good job, God!"

I'm sure David also experienced a sense of anticipation and waiting from the time he was anointed as the next king of Israel until the time he actually took his place on the throne. David experienced a range of emotions in the form of fear, pressure, anger, anxiety and more when he was forced out of Israel, on the run from Saul, fighting battles and surviving in a harsh land. But even in the midst of such adversity, it says in 2 Samuel 3:1 that "David grew stronger and stronger, while the house of Saul grew weaker and weaker." Finally, it was time. In chapter 5, David and his men took the stronghold of Zion (Jerusalem) and defeated the Philistines to secure the city in which the Lord would build David's house.

The victory over the Philistines was significant not because it secured David's new place as king, but because David brought the presence of God (the Ark of the Covenant) out of the hands of the Philistines and into the midst of His people. The prize for David's many years of waiting was the presence of the almighty God, rather than the presentation of a crown. David's response was nothing short of inspiring.

"Wearing a linen ephod, David was dancing before the Lord with all his might, while he and all Israel were bringing up the ark of the Lord with shouts and the sound of trumpets" (2 Sam. 6:14-15). He worshiped undignified, unfiltered and unashamed. The weight of the wait was over and David found himself caught up in the moment, liberated by the joy of being in the presence of God.

Do you ever feel the weight of the wait upon you? Maybe you feel the shame of being let go from a job, exhaustion of fighting night and day against the ever present voice of "mom guilt," the anger of waiting on a promise that isn't yet fulfilled or the fear of not knowing what's going to happen to your child. David waited years to bring the presence of God to Israel, but because of Jesus, we can experience hope, freedom, joy and security in the presence of God always.

**Because of God's presence, we can release the weight of the wait and be fully present.**

Friend, what things are keeping you from being in the moment today? What is the weight you are carrying? God sees you, He knows you and He wants to offer you freedom in the place of fear and pressure, joy in the place of anger and security in the place of anxiety.

So, as the things of your life threaten to overtake you, take a moment to look to Jesus and let his presence bring you back to a place of liberating joy.

# WEEK EIGHTEEN

18

## *REVELATION*

2 SAMUEL 11-12

2 SAMUEL 13, 15

2 SAMUEL 18-19

2 SAMUEL 24, PSALM 1

PSALM 23, PSALM 139

**MEMORY VERSE**

"SEARCH ME, GOD, AND KNOW MY HEART; TEST ME AND KNOW MY ANXIOUS THOUGHTS. SEE IF THERE IS ANY OFFENSIVE WAY IN ME, AND LEAD ME IN THE WAY EVERLASTING."

**PSALM 139:23-24**

# DANGEROUS PRAYERS

**BY JESSICA PARKER**

*"Search me, God, and know my heart; test me and know my anxious thoughts. See if there is any offensive way in me, and lead me in the way everlasting"* (Ps. 139:23-24, emphasis added).

I prayed this prayer at the beginning of 2022 while I was participating in a ten day prayer and fasting challenge. Shortly after, I started noticing things about myself that I didn't like. Things in my life that I thought I had already dealt with. Things in myself that I would rather keep hidden, such as my obsession with appearances, the short temper I tend to get with my kids, judgment, pride, and the bitterness in my heart towards someone that I have carried for too long.

When I first started seeing these things within me clearly, my thoughts jumped to "God how can this be? I felt like I was growing closer to you and strengthening my relationship with you. Now I see all these sins evident in my life." I felt defeated and unworthy. Then I felt the Spirit say, "This is what you prayed for; now let me help you."

As David cried out in Psalm 139, with desperation to grow closer to God, we, too, can do the same. If we truly mean the prayer, we have to understand that we will probably not like the results. How are we to recognize hidden sin unless God points it out? If God never revealed the sin in our life that we try so hard to cover up, then how would we be able to fix it?

These revelations of sin don't make us more distant from God, but rather is what is needed for us to recognize how we still have a ways to go. He does not reveal it to us to condemn us or make us hate ourselves. Instead, He does it to set us free and draw us closer to him. **Confession, repentance and reconciliation brings us into a deeper relationship with God.**

Confession, repentance and reconciliation bring us into a deeper relationship with God.

Those revelations scared me at first, and made me feel unworthy; however, I am now thankful for them. Because now that I am more aware, I can repent and ask for forgiveness. I can also be more mindful of when I am tempted in the areas that have been revealed and ask the Holy Spirit to guide me. This acknowledgement, confession, repentance, and reconciliation has continued to draw me closer to God.

Christ is truly with us to lead us, heal us, and forgive us. We are not called to dwell in our sins and past mistakes, this only further discourages us. Instead, we are called to dwell in the love of Jesus and allow Him to lead us in the way everlasting. After all, He is the One who has paid for all sin.

Trust me, I know this is a dangerous prayer, but I encourage you to ask the Holy Spirit to guide you through these last two verses of Psalm 139. This prayer has only deepened my relationship with our Heavenly Father. Invite the investigation of your innermost self. Ask Him to reveal the things that you may not even know about yourself. No matter what He reveals to you, and how hard it is to see, He will be faithful to lead you in the way everlasting. To Him you are completely worth it, so much so that He gave His life for you.

# WEEK NINETEEN

*JOY*

PSALM 119:1-80

PSALM 119:81-176

1 KINGS 1-2

1 KINGS 3, 4:29-34

1 KINGS 5:13-7:1

## MEMORY VERSE

"TROUBLE AND DISTRESS HAVE COME UPON ME,
BUT YOUR COMMANDS GIVE ME DELIGHT."

PSALM 119:143

# FROM TRIALS TO TRIUMPH

**BY JANNETTA COX**

Every mother dreams of the moment that they can snuggle and bond with their baby after the height of labor. After twelve hours of labor and a third degree tear, I was more than ready. I will never forget the anticipation as I sat in my wheelchair, holding my bundle of joy, waiting to be transferred to a normal room. It was only a few short minutes later that my doctor came in to tell me that wasn't happening. In the next few moments, she explained that my blood pressure had risen to an extremely high level and if they didn't treat it immediately, I could end up having a seizure. What I later learned is that I had postpartum preeclampsia. Postpartum preeclampsia is a serious condition that if not treated could cause a stroke, brain damage, and death. Moments later, I was back in the hospital bed being poked and prodded with IV's and a plethora of other devices.

I was devastated. How could such a beautiful moment take such a drastic turn? Momentarily, I gave in to what felt like such a traumatic experience but shortly afterwards, I was reminded of God's word. I will never forget the verses I meditated on leading up to childbirth such as James 1:2, "Consider it pure joy, my brothers and sisters, whenever you face trials of many kinds, because you know that the testing of your faith produces perseverance." When the Holy Spirit brought this to my remembrance, I felt joy in knowing that even in the trials I was facing, I would persevere because God's word promises our trial will produce something beautiful in us. The more I held on to God's word, not only was I healing physically but also spiritually.

Did you know that if you allow God's Word to take root inside of you, you too can experience joy in the midst of tough circumstances?

We read in Psalm 119, "Trouble and distress have come upon me, but your commands give me delight" (Ps. 119:143). In this passage, we see the fruit of joy and perseverance from the psalmist as he expresses the love he has for God's Word in in spite of tough times. Interestingly enough, Psalm 119 is the longest chapter in the Bible. And in this chapter, we see just how much the psalmist allowed God's Word to take root on the inside. More importantly, the psalmist doesn't ignore his troubles, but finds joy in God's commands *in spite of them.*

In the Bible, we see several examples of the importance of the Word of God. We also find that if we cling to His commands, it can produce good fruit in our lives as it did for the psalmist. For example in Luke 8, Jesus tells the parable of the sower to a large crowd. As the seed was scattered, it was only the seed that fell on good soil that produced a crop. He further explains the parable to the disciples by revealing this seed represents God's word. Luke 8:15 states, "'but the seed on good soil stands for those with a noble and good heart, who hear the word, retain it, and by persevering produce a crop."

In times of trouble, find joy in the Word of God and hold tight to His commands, knowing He will produce, in your life, the fruit of perseverance. I will be the first to admit I haven't always done this. It is very tempting to get distracted by the weight of life. So much so, that we forget all God has commanded us in His Word. However, as believers we too must find delight in his commands in spite of hard circumstances. **Joy comes from the assurance of God's presence even in the midst of hard circumstances.**

I encourage you to take inventory of your life. As you take inventory, think about a tough moment you are currently experiencing. We all experience them. Now, I challenge you to take it to God's word. What does His Word say about it? Allow that Word to transform how you see your circumstance. As you spend this time with him, you will find a joy that will resonate through any trial.

"Joy comes from the assurance of God's presence even in the midst of hard circumstances."

# WEEK TWENTY

## *GOODNESS*

1 KINGS 8-9:9, 10:1-13

1 KINGS 11, PROVERBS 1

PROVERBS 2-3

PROVERBS 8, 31

1 KINGS 12, 13

**MEMORY VERSE**

"DO NOT WITHHOLD GOOD FROM THOSE TO WHOM
IT IS DUE, WHEN IT IS IN YOUR POWER TO ACT."

**PROVERBS 3:27**

# THE POWER TO SHOWER GOODNESS

## BY DANA SCHAEFER

"Why did she give this to me?" I heard a loved one ask as I left the room to attend to my baby upstairs. This was a knitted blanket I had made for his birthday gift that he had just unwrapped. Here's the blanket's backstory. His wife had assured me that he would "just love" a hand-knit blanket as a special gift from me the previous year. Believing her, I went to work selecting an attractive pattern and colorful, soft yarns. I worked on it late at night when my infant was sleeping. It took me over six months of late night knitting and over $300 of expensive yarns to create this large, cozy blanket. Overhearing his disdainful question as I climbed the stairs, I felt that my time and effort was not appreciated. The comment still hurts as I recall it well over a decade later.

Consider this contrasting scenario.

"Your eyebrows look really good today," were the parting words on a Zoom meeting I had recently with a female colleague. Of course, I thanked her before we said goodbye and closed the meeting app. Her words stuck with me. I got up from my desk and went to the bathroom to look in the mirror. My eyebrows looked okay to me. I did not see anything special, but I thought about her words for the rest of the afternoon. She took less than three seconds to speak the words out loud and they made a positive impact that lasted for days.

These two stories have one thing in common. Both focus on spoken words that made a lasting impact. King Solomon started the collection of maxims which became the book of Proverbs to keep wise sayings in one place, much like a catalog of wisdom. His desire was for his spoken words to be remembered and have a lasting impact. 1 Kings 4:29 tells us, "God gave Solomon wisdom and very great insight, and a breadth of understanding as measureless as the sand on the seashore." One-third of the book of Proverbs is framed as advice a father offers to a son, a parent to a child. Much of that advice is focused on how a wise person treats other people.

Heeding biblical advice shows strength of character. To strengthen character and to build healthy relationships, Proverbs 3:27 advises, "Do not withhold good from those to whom it is due, when it is in your power to act." Both comments spoken to me in the stories above made an impact. But only one made a good impact on my heart and brightened my day.

Has someone ever done something for you that made a lasting impression? Maybe they complimented a skill you possess. Or perhaps noticed a positive change or habit you were implementing. Or maybe it was something simple like, "Your hair looks good today."

**You have the power to shower goodness on everyone God puts in your path.**

This proverb offers a greater challenge. Think about the people you encounter on a daily basis. Some of them may live inside your house, others you may encounter in person outside your home, or even virtually.

Can you be the kind of woman who seizes brief moments to make a positive impact on others by offering a simple compliment or positive observation? Solomon, the wise king, thought this was good advice. Take his guidance to heart and do not withhold goodness from others. A well-spoken, timely word can change someone's day!

"You have the power to shower goodness on everyone God puts in your path."

# 21

## WEEK TWENTY-ONE

### PERSPECTIVE

1 KINGS 14, 16:29-17:24

1 KINGS 18-19

1 KINGS 21-22

1 KINGS 2-3

2 KINGS 4-5, 6:1-23

## MEMORY VERSE

"SINCE, THEN, YOU HAVE BEEN RAISED WITH
CHRIST, SET YOUR HEARTS ON THINGS ABOVE,
WHERE CHRIST IS, SEATED AT THE RIGHT HAND OF
GOD. SET YOUR MINDS ON THINGS ABOVE, NOT ON
EARTHLY THINGS."

COLOSSIANS 3:1-2

# WHISPERS OF PURPOSE

**BY BRITTANY MARLOW**

What I wanted most when I grew up, was to be a wife and a mom. God was gracious enough to allow that to become my reality but in the midst of the postpartum struggle with my first daughter, I felt a longing for something more. I thought maybe I needed a new job and prayed for God to bless me with a new title. One where I could say I'm a mom but I'm also *insert fancy job title here.* I prayed and searched, and that job with a shiny new name placard never came.

While waiting, I joined a Bible study group with a group of women who started to encourage me on a whole new level. As I rooted myself in His Word, dreams I didn't know I had started to unfold.

Recently, my daughter's class was asked to dress up for community helper day as something they would like to be when they grow up. My darling first born baby girl thought for a while and said she wanted to go to school dressed just like me, a mommy. That's when God whispered, "I've already given you one." He was referring to the fancy title I'd asked Him for. God knew I didn't need a new job or title; I needed a different perspective: His perspective.

In 1 Kings, Elijah was fearless in approaching the king and stayed steadfast in his calling from the Lord. Elijah just defeated the Baal priests, but Jezebel became enraged at this and threatened his life. Fearfully, Elijah ran. In his weakest moment, God not only provided food and drink, but also called out to him, "What are you doing here, Elijah?" (1 Kings 19:9). Elijah was ready to throw in the towel, completely defeated. Elijah answered, "I have been very zealous for the Lord God of Armies, but the Israelites have abandoned your covenant, torn down your altars, and killed your prophets with the sword. I alone am left, and they're looking for me to take my life" (1 Kings 19:14).

> "Instead of asking for a change in circumstance, pray for a change in perspective."

Elijah waited for a tremendous answer like he had previously received, but that's not what came. God brought mighty winds, an earthquake and a blazing fire, but His voice was heard in the small, gentle whisper. God's whisper and signs were the encouragement Elijah needed to hear and see from God's perspective. His confidence came from God and God alone. Nothing in this world can sustain us other than our God. The Lord asked him once more, "What are you doing here, Elijah?" (1 Kings 19:13). Elijah felt God's presence with him and he was humbled. His words were the same and his situation unchanged but he was renewed by hearing God's voice. God's whisper helped Elijah exchange his doubt for trust.

Elijah was waiting for God to answer him with a miracle; instead, He sent Elijah a whisper. He didn't change his path or his calling. He gave Elijah a shift in perspective. Through that seemingly small answer, Elijah remembered his God given purpose. He was confident and courageous again. He rested in his confirmation from the Lord.

**Instead of asking for a change in circumstance, pray for a change in perspective.** Pray for your doubt to be exchanged for trust in the Lord's unfailing love and promises. I encourage you to shift your perspective of how you view yourself to the same lens God uses. The deeper I become rooted in God's Word, the easier it becomes to step into the identity of who God says I am and to step out of the identity of who the world says I am. God has given you an assignment and if you're listening, you'll find guidance and confirmation in His sweet whispers.

# R.O.O.T.

## JOURNALING GUIDE

It's one thing to read God's Word; it's another thing to actually *understand* and *apply* it.

Move from information to practical application with our tried-and-true R.O.O.T. study method. Use your journal to walk through the following steps for each day's reading:

### READ

Read the passage of Scripture, highlighting or underlining any words or phrases that stick out to you.

### OWN WORDS

Shorten the overall story or message into your own words.

### OBSERVE

Jot down your observations. Here are some questions to get you started—
- What part of today's reading stood out to you the most, and why?
- What do we know about the author of this book?
- When was this book written, and what was happening at this time in Israel's history?
- Is there a promise or prophecy that Jesus fulfilled?
- Is there a person (or people) you relate to in this passage?
- Was there anything you didn't understand?*

### TAKEAWAY

Think about what you read today, as it relates to your own life—
- How do these truths impact the way I see Jesus?
- How do these truths impact the way I see others?
- How do these truths impact the way I see myself?
- How do these truths impact the way I see my current life situation(s)?

What action is the Holy Spirit leading you to take based on what you wrote down?

*We love the Enduring Word Commentary for all those hard-to-understand moments in Scripture!
Visit www.enduringword.com or download the app for quick and easy access.*

# WEEK
# TWENTY-TWO

## CORRECTION

JONAH 1-2

JONAH 3-4

HOSEA 1-2

HOSEA 3, 6

HOSEA 11, 14

**MEMORY VERSE**

"YOU, LORD, ARE FORGIVING AND GOOD,
ABOUNDING IN LOVE TO ALL WHO CALL YOU."

**PSALM 86:5**

# GRACEFUL ACCOUNTABILITY

**BY FAITH SPEARMAN**

Looking down at the bathroom floor, now fairly covered in bath water, I turned to my toddler, "Matthew, Mama just got done telling you not to do that." Recently, I found myself having to take a lot of deep breaths, eyes closed, and whisper, "Lord, help me."

He'd taken a liking to "baking" during his bath time and would insist, in his own nonverbal way, that he needed the tools to do so. As he'd fill his mixing bowl with "batter," he'd often dump it over the side of the tub.

As most mamas do, I'd find myself wondering if I was being firm enough, giving an abundance of verbal warnings, or too firm, having to, at times, resort to simply removing the problematic vessel: the mixing bowl. In which case, even with the promise of the return of the bowl once the lesson was learned, I was met with alligator tears and toddler sized rebuke. Most often, after the tears subsided and the understanding took over, this was quickly followed with repentant remorse in the form of a tiny kiss or tender "pat-pat-pat" on the leg. On other occasions, the response was less desirable, ending in a full-blown tantrum. And in these moments of varying emotions, I'd often find myself looking at this little being and wondering if God ever felt this way.

In the book of Hosea, we see a pattern of sin that isn't met with immediate remorse. The Lord created a parallel, portraying the stubborn unfaithfulness of God's chosen children, the Israelites. Hosea was instructed to marry Gomer, an unfaithful woman, and have children. Each child named by the Lord in warning of the punishment the Israelites would suffer as a result of their unfaithfulness. Just as Gomer abandoned Hosea, the Israelites had abandoned God, adopting the idols of the Canaanites and turning from the ways of the Lord. Their repentance was slow to manifest, not coming to actualization, but the vision of what their repentance would look like being beautifully illustrated in Hosea 14, "People will dwell again in his shade, they will flourish like the grain, they will blossom like the vine - Israel's fame will be like the wine of Lebanon." (v.7)

A promise of restoration from a Father with a loving, gracious heart, even in the midst of their sin, "I will heal their waywardness and love them freely, for my anger has turned away from them" (Hos. 14:3).

In the Israelites' sin, the Lord's love was still evident; He still foreshadowed the blessings the Israelites would find in returning to Him while never wavering in the correction He's always faithful to give.

What we see following all of this sin is the posture of His heart for us. The evidence that His heart is never for our destruction, but only for our good, because His love is never far removed even in His loving correction. Even when we're running in every direction but towards Him, He desires for us to experience the promises of a life lived in righteous repentance.

Friends, when we find ourselves toe-to-toe with disobedience, like the Israelites, be reminded of what repentance can look like. We, too, need to be held accountable, that in our own sin repentance must be absolute. **Remember, God's love is never absent, even in the midst of the consequences.** When we find ourselves in a state of awareness of our own sin, it allows for the fullness of His love that's in us, through His Holy correction, to extend to those around us, whether it be in the wake of repeated offense or something so seemingly harmless as bathwater on the bathroom floor. Through this, may we be quickened to have the very same heart, mirroring His own in ushering graceful accountability.

Even when there is no immediate relent in offense, be gracious of heart, not failing to show the love and mercy we so often receive, but maintaining accountability and extending His promises that are held in divine correction.

---

"Remember, God's love is never absent, even in the midst of the consequences."

# 23

## WEEK
## TWENTY-THREE

### CALLED

ISAIAH 6, 11

ISAIAH 40-41

ISAIAH 43, 45

ISAIAH 51, 53

ISAIAH 55, 61

## MEMORY VERSE

"...FOR IT IS GOD WHO WORKS IN YOU TO WILL
AND TO ACT IN ORDER TO FULFILL HIS GOOD
PURPOSE."

**PHILIPPIANS 2:13**

# "HERE I AM, SEND ME"

## BY JOAN LAVORI

When my children were young, I attended a group for mothers. I had great support; I made friends. My kids had a great time and we were fed with the word of God. Then, I was asked to consider leading the group. My immediate answer was, "No! I am not qualified!" I was asked to pray about it, and to see where God would lead.

I sought God through His Word and through prayer. I felt unworthy and prideful in thinking that if I were to lead this group, it would be in my own strength. I was forced to confess the sin of pride and ask for God's forgiveness. As 1 John 1:9 says, "If we confess our sins, He is faithful and just and will forgive us our sins and purify us from all unrighteousness." God graciously allowed me to see that my strength was in my willingness to say "yes" to His call.

In Isaiah 6:1-4, Isaiah saw God in all His glory, and he was overwhelmed! How could he, a sinful man, living among a disobedient, sinful people (the people of Judah), see the King, the Lord Almighty, and live? Recognizing his unworthiness, Isaiah cried out, "Woe to me! I am ruined" (Is. 6:5). Yet, because of God's great love for His children, He transforms us and makes us worthy (2 Thess. 1:11). He did this for Isaiah and He continues to do this for everyone who calls Him "Abba Father."

Isaiah's response to the Lord's voice saying, "Whom shall I send? And who will go for us?" (Is. 6:8) was immediate. Without knowing what he was being asked to do, or where he was being sent, he responded, "Here am I, Send me" (Is. 6:8). Having experienced God's love and mercy, he no longer felt inadequate. He was ready to answer God's call.

You, too, have probably struggled with answering God's call to serve Him. We want to know the minutest details. Where? When? How? Are we qualified? In evaluating my qualifications or "worthiness" to answer God's call, I was looking at the things the world told me I needed: experience, a perfect family, to be "good enough." You probably have a similar list.

However, God sees us so differently from the way we see ourselves.

"In Christ, we are competent for every calling."

In His eyes, we are worthy because He has made us worthy; the blood that Jesus shed on the cross qualifies us. We need only to have hearts that are willing to do His will. The rest is up to Him.

**In Christ, we are competent for every calling.**

I thank God for calling me to serve Him for those three years. I was blessed by the women we served, and those that I served alongside. We saw God at work in our families. My children were nurtured in God's word, and that has been foundational in their lives. I am still friends with many of the moms from my group. I would have missed a great blessing had I said, "No," to serving God.

Is God calling you? Do you hear His faint whisper calling you to step out in faith? Friend, even though you and I may not have a vision of the Almighty as Isaiah did, He still calls us to do His will. Let us put aside our reservations and our reasons, so that we may answer faithfully and boldly as Isaiah did, "Here am I. Send me" (Is. 6:8).

# WEEK TWENTY-FOUR

### ROOTED

2 KINGS 17-18

2 KINGS 19-20

2 KINGS 22-23

2 KINGS 24-25

JEREMIAH 1, 17

## MEMORY VERSE

"'BUT BLESSED IS THE ONE WHO TRUSTS IN THE LORD, WHOSE CONFIDENCE IS IN HIM. THEY WILL BE LIKE A TREE PLANTED BY THE WATER THAT SENDS OUT ITS ROOTS BY THE STREAM. IT DOES NOT FEAR WHEN HEAT COMES; ITS LEAVES ARE ALWAYS GREEN. IT HAS NO WORRIES IN A YEAR OF DROUGHT AND NEVER FAILS TO BEAR FRUIT.'"

**JEREMIAH 17:7-8**

# WHERE ARE YOU ROOTED?

**BY KATIE GIBSON**

The summer sun beat down oppressively, as I walked and processed the latest COVID-19 update. My kids wouldn't be going back to school, in person, as planned. *Sigh.* By now we were getting used to disappointment.

I thought about the days ahead— of endless virtual calls, dozens of log-in passwords to keep track of, and math problems I wasn't qualified enough to solve. I thought about the "baby" ministry under my care, and all the meetings and tasks that entailed. I thought about all the work travel my husband had coming up, that would take him away from home. As I considered all these things, I began to feel completely and utterly overwhelmed.

"I can't do this," I told Jesus, hot tears stinging my eyes. My conclusion was final: He must intervene in my situation, or I would certainly be done for.

As I continued, my path took me beside the lake near our house, where well-established trees towered over the muddied waters. My eyes studied their branches, stretched high and wide, prompting a familiar scripture to come to mind: "...Blessed is the one who trusts in the Lord, *whose confidence is in him.* They will be like a tree planted by the water that sends out its roots by the stream. It does not fear..." (Jer. 17:7-8, emphasis added).

In the chapters surrounding this simile, Jeremiah rebukes the nation of Israel. They were stuck in a cycle of sin and doomed for destruction, so the young prophet gets down to the literal root of the problem: confidence in themselves instead of trusting God.

Yahweh had called Israel out of slavery in Egypt, then led them into the desert to learn how to live a life of dependence on Him. After 40 years of wandering, they had (mostly) learned their lesson. However, after they entered the Promised Land, old habits soon returned. God had chosen them to be "oaks of righteousness, a planting of the LORD for the display of his splendor" (Is. 61:3). Instead, they became like a "stunted shrub in the desert" (Jer. 17:6 NLT), worthless and doomed to destruction.

Jehovah Jireh was, and is, more than enough for His people's every need. But, in their pride, Israel traded His abundant provision opting to strive in their own ability.

God took the Israelites back out of their land and into exile to reiterate His original lesson. In the same way, he leads you and I into "desert seasons" to remind us to place and keep our total confidence rooted in Him.

That hot summer day by the lake, I had a choice to make: I could grin and bear the coming days in my own strength (which would surely lead to burnout) or I could place my confidence solely in Christ and trust Him to be enough for every moment. Thankfully, I chose the latter. When I look back on that season, now, all I can see is grace and more grace. I can say, with the psalmist David, "...those who seek the Lord lack no good thing" (Ps. 34:10).

Friend, He won't fail you either. He is worthy of all our trust. Are you facing a situation that feels impossible? Are you fearful and frustrated when it comes to finances, parenting, or something else?

The feeling of "not enough" is a sure-fire sign that we're putting confidence in our own ability instead of God's. **When we are rooted in Christ alone, we can rest in the knowledge that He is sufficient for every situation.**

Right now, allow the Holy Spirit to reveal any area where you've been rooted in self-confidence, then confess the sin of pride; "He is faithful and just and *will* forgive" (1 Jn. 1:9, emphasis added). Turn from your own strength, your own ideas, or even your own righteousness. Commit to live each day rooted in complete dependence on Christ. *He is the Well that never runs dry.*

---

"When we are rooted in Christ alone, we can rest in the knowledge that He is sufficient for every situation."

# WEEK TWENTY-FOUR TAKEAWAY

# 25

## WEEK TWENTY-FIVE

### *RESTORATION*

JEREMIAH 23, 25

JEREMIAH 29, 33

EZEKIEL 34, 37

DANIEL 1-2

DANIEL 3-4

## MEMORY VERSE

"BEAR FRUIT IN KEEPING WITH REPENTANCE."

### MATTHEW 3:8

# REBELLIOUS TO RESTORED

## BY KERYN STOKES

For much of my young life, I lived in such a way that would be considered a "backslidden" Christian. I partied every weekend, missed church more than I attended, and my life revolved around my desires - not God's. I had the knowledge of the Gospel. I believed Jesus to be the Son of God, and I'd even tell people about Him, but my actions did not line up with that of a Christian.

In this week's reading, specifically in Jeremiah, we see how the people of Judah were not facing exile to Babylon for their lack of knowledge of the truth. Jeremiah 25:4-5 says, "Again and again the Lord has sent you his servants, the prophets, but you have not listened or even paid attention. Each time the message was this: 'Turn from the evil road you are traveling and from the evil things you are doing.'" Rather, it was their willful rebellion that saw God's judgment befall them. God was patient (like, 900 years patient) and by this time had given His people every opportunity to repent, yet they resisted and continued to live according to their own way. Personally, I resonated with these passages.

Although I lived in a similar rebellion as the Israelites, today I consider myself fortunate to know the transformative power of the love of God and what He's done for us by sending Jesus Christ to die on the cross. After years of living recklessly, it was one decision that would transform me into an obedient, disciplined, and devoted Christian. What was that decision? Repentance! True, utter, repentance of my grievous sinful nature, finally laid at the foot of the cross for once and for all. Not to be picked up again when I felt sad, or when I had a bad day, but never to be touched again.

**Repentance is more than asking for forgiveness or feeling sorry, it requires action.** Like a father might let his children go in the way of their poor decisions, so did God when He sent the Israelites to Babylon. God did this with the hope that they would come to their own conclusion towards repentance. The Hebrew verb we translate repentance means "to return."*

*Wieja, Estera. "What Did Jesus Mean by Repent? The Hebrew Meaning of Teshuva." 3 August 2021, https://firmisrael.org/learn/what-did-jesus-mean-by-repent-the-hebrew-meaning-of-teshuva/.

"Repentance is more than asking for forgiveness or feeling sorry, it requires action."

Just as God was looking for His people to return to Him and His law, He looks for us to return to Him through His son, Jesus Christ.

Jeremiah's prophecies made it clear that a new covenant would be established with God's people! The good news is already here, friends. Let us not be exiled, but let us return to the cross in humble repentance.

The first step to repentance is admitting it needs to happen. Don't be discouraged along the way for "we all fall short of the glory of God" (Rom. 3:23), but be glad! It is God who is shedding light on our sin, not to condemn us, but to bring us closer to Himself.

After admittance, ask for forgiveness, and move forward anew. Be patient with yourself during the daily process that is changing your lifestyle, your habits, and even your thoughts. Rely on God and His restoring power.

He isn't content to leave us in broken conditions and it can be said that spiritual growth is forever, even on the other side of the cross. What a beautiful future for us to constantly live and strive towards.

One pattern that you've probably noticed throughout the Old Testament is that the Israelites often gathered to retell and remember the story of God's faithfulness to them as a nation. This retelling and remembering was imperative to fuel their faith in and commitment to Yahweh.

You and I have a story too, and it's not limited to our conversion experience. It is important for us to recognize, document, and share with the next generation those seasons where we can look back and trace God's hand.

Revisit Joshua 24:1-13 to read an example of the Israelites' testimony. Then, prayerfully take some time to write down important "markers" along your faith journey.

_____

_____

_____

_____

_____

_____

_____

_____

_____

_____

_____

_____

_____

_____

_____

_____

_____

_____

_____

_____

_____

_____

_____

_____

_____

_____

_____

_____

_____

_____

_____

_____

_____

_____

_____

_____

_____

_____

_____

_____

_____

## Continue the story...

Make a regular habit of journaling to capture God's faithfulness in your life. Write down prayer requests, current challenges, and what God is speaking. Later you'll be able to go back and see how He has answered prayers, opened and shut doors, and directed you through still, small whispers. Your children and grandchildren can read those stories one day, too, and be encouraged to trust God in every season.

# WEEK
# TWENTY-SIX

### HOME

DANIEL 5-6

DANIEL 9-10

EZRA 1-2

EZRA 3-4

EZRA 5-6

## MEMORY VERSE

"AND I PRAY THAT YOU, BEING ROOTED AND
ESTABLISHED IN LOVE, MAY HAVE POWER,
TOGETHER WITH ALL THE LORD'S HOLY
PEOPLE, TO GRASP HOW WIDE AND LONG AND
HIGH AND DEEP IS THE LOVE OF CHRIST."

**EPHESIANS 3:17B-18**

# HOME IS WHERE THE HEART IS

**BY LONETTE M. BAITY**

Have you ever felt stuck? Not the feeling you get after a bad attempt at parallel parking. I mean truly trapped in a life you didn't ask for - no way back and unsure how to move forward?

When my family moved to South Carolina from Ohio, I left behind everything and every person I had ever known. Within six months of our move, my marriage disintegrated; I was unemployed and pregnant with a fourth child.

In my despair, I would take my kindergartner to school, set my toddler and preschooler down to watch PBS kids and climb back into bed. With a hand on my swollen belly, a pillow catching the tears from my puffy eyes, I felt like an orphan. I was afraid of the future and trapped in the present with no real place to call home.

Even in those moments, God's word flooded my soul. He reminded me that I abide in Him. And My heart, albeit broken, was still beating.

God's steadfast love remained and sustained me.
He became the bedrock of my existence.

When I read about Ezra (Ezra 1-6) and the captives taken into Babylon in this week's passages, I imagine they felt something like this. Not only had their homes been lost, but the temple - God's house - had also been destroyed. There was no going back to the way things were. The grief must have been overwhelming. I'm sure the thought of rebuilding their lives after such devastation seemed like an impossible and frightening task but God's people were able to push past the fear and begin the healing process. Ezra 3:3 explains, "Despite their fear of the peoples around them, they built the altar on its foundation and sacrificed burnt offerings on it to the Lord, both the morning and evening sacrifices."

As days turned into weeks, weeks turned into months, God brought His people hope of restoration and reminded them that their true home was found in Him.

# "In broken places, God's love becomes our home."

In His unfailing love, God gave them the courage to rebuild the broken places and inhabit the promised land again. Eventually, the temple was rebuilt, and the priests and Levites once again served the Lord: "When the builders laid the foundation of the temple of the Lord, the priests in their vestments and with trumpets, and the Levites (the sons of Asaph) with cymbals, took their places to praise the Lord, as prescribed by David king of Israel" (Ezra 3:10).

As you read the story of Ezra and the captives, you may find your story written on the pages, too. You are not abandoned, dear Sister. Here, is where we press into the faithfulness of God. We can face opposition with the comfort of knowing we place our hope in Him and in his love.

Ezra 3:11 reminds us of his unfailing love. "With praise and thanksgiving they sang to the Lord: 'He is good; his love toward Israel endures forever!'" And all the people gave a great shout of praise to the Lord, because the foundation of the house of the Lord was laid."

Slowly, but with a steady hand and a strong arm, God gives courage and strength to rebuild His house - even if it is our broken hearts. He fills in the empty spaces. And the broken spaces that are still healing just serve as conduits of compassion to leak love to others.

**In broken places, God's love becomes our home.** He did it for Israel. He did it for me. He can do it for you.

In your prayer time today, ask the Holy Spirit to stir your memories to see God's faithful love over the past 60 days. Start with a list of just 3-4 and post it in a place where you can see it. It could be directly from scripture or indirectly from people He has brought to you! As you remember His faithfulness, let your heart find its home in His love.

# WEEK TWENTY-SEVEN

2 7

## DEVOTION

EZRA 7-8

EZRA 9-10

ESTHER 1-2

ESTHER 3-4

ESTHER 5-6

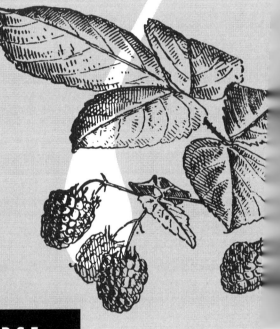

## MEMORY VERSE

"AND MAY YOUR HEARTS BE FULLY COMMITTED
TO THE LORD OUR GOD, TO LIVE BY HIS DECREES
AND OBEY HIS COMMANDS, AS AT THIS TIME."

### 1 KINGS 8:61

# WATERED-DOWN DEVOTION

**BY KATIE GIBSON**

My teenage son stared, disappointed, as he swirled his not-so-iced vanilla latte in front of him. We had stopped for coffee before a doctor's appointment, but he had been so fixated on filling his stomach with food that he never got around to enjoying his beverage. Hours later, the cup was now covered in condensation. Inside, tiny shards of ice floated around in the noticeably lighter liquid. The once-desirable drink was now completely unappetizing.

God knew the same thing would happen to His family if they intermarried with other nations. He had chosen the nation of Israel to display His glory to the world, through them. He called them to be different, set apart. God's directives on intermarrying had nothing to do with race and everything to do with their wholeheartedness.

God explained, through Moses, "Do not intermarry... they will turn your children away from following me to serve other gods, and the Lord's anger will burn against you and will quickly destroy you" (Deut. 7:3-4).

And of course God was right. Years later, Solomon "loved many foreign women" (1 Kings 11:1). His compromise started a Domino effect.

Israel was led astray to worship other gods in addition to Yahweh. Their spiritual devotion became so watered down they looked and lived no different than anyone else. The nation that once was a clear display of God's might and splendor experienced drought, famine, and eventually exile.

This history explains Ezra's extreme reaction to the report of intermarriage after returning home to Jerusalem. As a priest and student of the Torah, he immediately perceived the danger of their disobedience of God's command.

Ezra grieved. Ezra prayed. And the Word says, "a large crowd... gathered around him" (Ezra 10:1). Together they wept over their unfaithfulness to their faithful God. But they didn't stop at confession— they truly repented by taking action. The foreigners willing to lay aside their nation's gods and embrace Yahweh as the one true God stayed, while everyone else was sent away.

As believers, we are chosen to live as salt in a tasteless world so that others will "taste and see that the Lord is good" (Ps. 34:8). To be salty requires that we be set apart, wholeheartedly devoted unto God's ways— not everyone else's.

Sadly, if we look around, we see a church that is not unlike that which Ezra saw. Like my son's latte and the Israelites, many of us have conformed to our environment. We have intermarried with the ways of the world:

- We worship materialistic things, pop stars, and political leaders.
- We determine "truth" by our feelings and popular opinion.
- We destroy relationships through selfishness and foolish arguments.

When we study God's Word, like Ezra, we see that God takes obedience seriously; as Christ-followers, we should too. His glory should be our utmost priority in everything we say and do.

**Intermarrying with the world's ways waters down our witness.** In response, we should all stop right here and ask ourselves this question: In what ways have I become conformed to my worldly environment?

When the Holy Spirit reveals an area of disobedience, take time to grieve and confess. But, friend, don't let it stop there— allow that grieving to move you to genuine repentance through action. Throw that addiction in the trash. Delete the app. Call a friend for accountability.

Wholehearted devotion concentrates God's "flavor" in our lives. Make the decision to "be fully committed to the Lord our God, to live by his decrees and obey his commands..." (1 Kings 8:61). When others "taste" your life, they will desire what's inside, and you can share with them your not-so-secret ingredient— Jesus.

---

"Intermarrying with the world's ways waters down our witness."

---

# WEEK
# TWENTY-EIGHT

## TROUBLE

ESTHER 7-8

ESTHER 9-10

NEHEMIAH 1-2

NEHEMIAH 3-4

NEHEMIAH 5-6

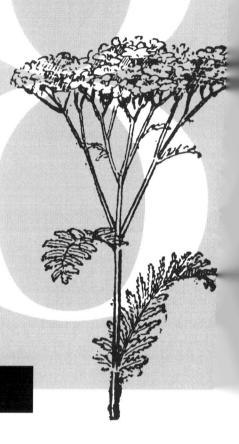

**MEMORY VERSE**

"I HAVE TOLD YOU THESE THINGS, SO THAT IN ME
YOU MAY HAVE PEACE. IN THIS WORLD YOU WILL
HAVE TROUBLE. BUT TAKE HEART! I HAVE
OVERCOME THE WORLD."

**JOHN 16:33**

# WHEN TROUBLE COMES

**BY LINDSAY MCNEELY**

I have always loved haunted mazes. In high school and college, my friends and I would make sure to visit our local corn maze each year. They built a massive and phenomenally scary haunted maze each October. It was a thrill to walk blindly in the dark not knowing when something or someone was going to jump out and frighten you. We would scream and we would laugh until we cried. It was thrilling because we knew it was not real. The things in that maze could not really cause us harm or distress.

Things are quite different in real life. Those things that come out of nowhere seem bigger and scarier. The darkness and the unknown do not bring laughs in the real world because they can become big things that harm us and cause us fear.

My husband and I are navigating the foster care system. We are currently completing all necessary steps to open our home for foster care. Our emotions have been on a wild roller coaster, and we know it will only speed up once a child is placed in our home. It seems that the questions pile up, the unknowns become scarier, and the what ifs grow larger each day.

Reading through Nehemiah, the account of the Israelites rebuilding the wall around Jerusalem spoke to my heart:

> So we continued the work with half the men holding spears, from the first light of dawn till the stars came out. At that time I also said to the people, "Have every man and his helper stay inside Jerusalem at night, so they can serve us as guards by night and as workers by day." Neither I nor my brothers nor my men nor the guards with me took off our clothes; each had his weapon, even when he went for water. (Nehemiah 4:21 - 23)

The people faced severe opposition. They had to work while holding weapons for protection. They labored day and night building and guarding. Do you ever feel the exhaustion of laboring day and night to work for and guard your family?

> "When life throws its taunts and fears our way, we can stand firm in God's calling and promises."

Nehemiah believed that God would see them through. Even through the opposition, the taunts, the fear, and the exhaustion, he placed his full trust in the Lord. Nehemiah knew the work God had called him to complete, and he knew God would provide if he was obedient.

Jesus knew the trouble we would face. He knew how hard and scary the world can be, but He left us with a promise. John 16:33 reminds us that this world will bring trouble, but Jesus has overcome the world. He is victorious!

When the world is dark and scary, we can place our trust in Jesus. When the path seems unclear, we can lean on Him. **When life throws its taunts and fears our way, we can stand firm in God's calling and promises.**

Nehemiah knew the trouble this world could bring, but just as Jesus promised, Nehemiah also knew that God would be victorious. My husband and I know that this path we are on will bring fear, pain, and sadness. However, we can stand firm just as Nehemiah and the people of Israel did with our weapon in one hand (God's very words and promises) while we continue the work the Lord has laid before us with the other hand.

Our God is faithful. He is working for our good and for His glory (Rom. 8:28). And He is victorious. Wherever He has called you, continue to fight clinging to His word and His promises as you continue in His work.

# WEEK TWENTY-EIGHT TAKEAWAY

# WEEK TWENTY-NINE

## REPENTANCE

NEHEMIAH 7-8

NEHEMIAH 9-10

NEHEMIAH 11-12

NEHEMIAH 13

MALACHI 3

## MEMORY VERSE

"HAVE MERCY ON ME, O GOD, ACCORDING TO YOUR UNFAILING LOVE; ACCORDING TO YOUR GREAT COMPASSION BLOT OUT MY TRANSGRESSIONS. WASH AWAY ALL MY INIQUITY AND CLEANSE ME FROM MY SIN."

**PSALM 51:1-2**

# DRAWN TO REPENTANCE

**BY JESS RIDGEWAY**

I had a youth leader who had this thing about God and a 2x4. She would tell us how in different seasons of her life it felt like God was smacking her over the head with it repeatedly. Got a lesson you really need to learn? Wham! 2x4. Oops, it didn't really sink in. Let's try again. Bam! 2x4. Every time she'd turn there was God showing her the same thing again until it sank down deep into her soul.

Well, as I've grown up I can see what she means. Do you want to know what God has been revealing to me lately? Really? Here you go: There is no good thing in me. *Ouch.*

But wait, I've always been a good girl, made responsible decisions, followed the rules; surely there's a little good, right? *Wham!* 2x4.

In the latter portions of Nehemiah, we get to see the newly restored Israelites studying scripture together. All of a sudden they are smacked with the truth about who God is and who they are. Their response? Mourning. Weeping. Sackcloth and ashes.

Chapter nine contains the longest prayer in the Bible. It is a confession that sums up the biblical narrative to this point. It contrasts God's faithfulness to Israel's rebellion. Time and again Israel fails but God shows up in steadfast love and mercy. The Israelites praying here did not cross the Red Sea. They didn't witness the plagues, the pillars of cloud and fire, or the miracles in the wilderness. They did not lift up the golden calf or kill the prophets. Yet, in verse 33 their prayer changes from "they" to "we." They say "for you have dealt faithfully and we have acted wickedly" (emphasis added).

The restored Israelites are counting themselves equal with their ancestors in failure, humbly taking responsibility for their sin, confessing that God is right and they are wrong. These men and women could have tried to shift the blame. After all, they were in exile, raised in a foreign land around foreign gods, born to people who had disobeyed God. But no, they added themselves to the narrative.

When we
truly
understand
God's Word,
it brings us to
our knees in
awe and
repentance.

**When we truly understand God's Word, it brings us to our knees in awe and repentance.** The Israelites left their time of study convicted to the point of grief, recognizing that there was no good in them. They set aside their pride, took responsibility for their sin, and confessed their failure. This in turn led them to renew their covenant with the Lord who had proved himself faithful time and again.

As we read and study God's very words, the Holy Spirit shines a revealing light on the deepest, darkest corners of our soul, revealing sin we often had no idea was lurking there. Then we get the wonderful opportunity to repent and confess our sin, allowing God to remove it from us and replace it with his unending, amazing grace day by day.

As you read this week, ask the Holy Spirit to open your eyes and penetrate your heart with the truth of who you are in your sinfulness and who God is in His holiness and goodness. Let it sink down deep into your soul.

Spend time on your knees in honest confession, taking responsibility for your sin and adding your name to the sorry tale of humanity rebelling against their wonderful Creator. Repent and turn to the arms of the Lord who is steadfast in his love and mercy.

After all, naturally there is no good thing in you. But bless the Lord! Through the cross, you can now walk under daily grace.

Wham! Covered by the blood of Jesus. *Boom!* Forgiven by the Father. *Bam!* Empowered by the Holy Spirit.

# R.O.O.T.

## JOURNALING GUIDE

It's one thing to read God's Word; it's another thing to actually *understand* and *apply* it.

Move from information to practical application with our tried-and-true R.O.O.T. study method. Use your journal to walk through the following steps for each day's reading:

### READ

Read the passage of Scripture, highlighting or underlining any words or phrases that stick out to you.

### OWN WORDS

Shorten the overall story or message into your own words.

### OBSERVE

Jot down your observations. Here are some questions to get you started—
- Who is the author of this book, and what do we know about their life, personality, and profession?
- What is Jesus saying or doing in this passage?
- What do Jesus' words and actions reveal about the Father?
- Is there an Old Testament prophecy fulfilled?
- Is there a command to obey?
- Did anything surprise or confuse you?*

### TAKEAWAY

Think about today's passages—
- What part of this passage stuck out to you the most, and why?
- Based on what you read, how can you follow Jesus more closely?

*We love the Enduring Word Commentary for all those hard-to-understand moments in Scripture!*
*Visit www.enduringword.com or download the app for quick and easy access.*

# WEEK THIRTY

## PROMISES

JOHN 1:1-14, LUKE 1-2:38

MATTHEW 1, LUKE 2:39-52, MATTHEW 2

MATTHEW 3, MARK 1, LUKE 3

MATTHEW 4, LUKE 4-5

JOHN 1:15-51, JOHN 2

## MEMORY VERSE

"IN HIM WAS LIFE, AND THAT LIFE WAS THE
LIGHT OF ALL MANKIND. THE LIGHT SHINES IN
THE DARKNESS, AND THE DARKNESS HAS NOT
OVERCOME IT."

**JOHN 1:4-5**

# PROMISES HELD IN THE DARK

**BY NANCY EHLINGER**

Several years ago during a very dark period of time in my life, I went to the beach on Good Friday and cried out for God to speak to me. I was a hot mess. I had plenty of people throwing advice my way. Darkness threatened to overwhelm me. Fear had begun to take root in my thoughts. Silence followed me home.

Easter morning I drug myself to church, plopped down in my seat, almost tuning out the message: Missing Your Miracle. Every word became a promise. God stepped into my mess and gave me a promise. He didn't give me a roadmap or an illustrated fairy tale. Instead, He became a light for me to follow. In John 1:4 we read, "In him (Jesus) was life, and that life was the light of all mankind. The light shines in the darkness, and the darkness has not overcome it."

Jesus' birth was a promise delivered. The prophets foretold his coming. The chief priests and teachers of the law knew well where the Messiah would be born. When asked by Herod, they immediately answered, with "In Bethlehem in Judea" (Matt. 2:5).

God chose to step into the middle of a dark world as a baby and become a light for us to follow. Roman rule had become oppressive and even the temple priests were not caring for their people. When the Magi told of a star, a light they were following, the very teachers who knew the promises chose to stay in Jerusalem.

The priests could recite the prophets' words. They knew. Yet, when the light came, when the Creator of everything showed up, they stayed home. They were comfortable in the dark. The priests knew the promise. They quoted the prophet, Micah, "for out of you will come a ruler who will shepherd my people Israel" (Matt. 2:6). They expected a savior that would ride in on a warhorse. They thought peace would come at the end of a sword. However, Jesus' peace comes through sacrifice, through love.

Like me, they had already defined how God would deliver his promise. They missed the miracle of Jesus because they weren't able to see past their own expectations.

**Follow Jesus' light out of your comfort zone to fully embrace His promises.**

God promised me a miracle that day. There wasn't a magic wand, sigh. I had to keep showing up. Every day for three years. I kept holding on. Even when it was still dark, the promise was still there. The Creator of the universe made a promise but I had to show up. I had to move out of the comfortable and into the hard.

Mary and Joseph had to push through their own fears to hold the promise, Immanuel, God with us. The shepherds, these uneducated shepherds, rushed to Bethlehem to see what the angel of the Lord had told them about. The Magi followed a light out of their world to worship a King they did not know.

Friend, I don't know what fear may be holding you captive. Or, the darkness that surrounds you. I do know he heard my cries and He promised to be with me. Have you been trying to define how God should deliver your miracle? God won't give you a roadmap but if you step out in faith, He will light your way one step at a time.

"Follow Jesus' light out of your comfort zone to fully embrace His promises."

# 31

## WEEK THIRTY-ONE

*LOVE*

JOHN 3-5

MATTHEW 12:1-21, MARK 2-3

LUKE 6, MATTHEW 5-6

MATTHEW 7-8:13, LUKE 7

MATTHEW 11, 12:22-50

## MEMORY VERSE

"A NEW COMMAND I GIVE YOU: LOVE ONE ANOTHER. AS I HAVE LOVED YOU, SO YOU MUST LOVE ONE ANOTHER."

**JOHN 13:34**

# RULES ARE MEANT TO BE BROKEN

**BY MARTHA RUDOLPH**

"Don't take my spot or anything on it!"

Sound familiar? Growing up, if we had to leave our seats during TV watching time, my brothers and I used to use that phrase to safeguard our space: the TV remote, pillows, blankets, really anything that was "'our spot" or "on it." We completely made up the rule, but we all took it seriously. If you forgot to "call your spot," the consequence was on your shoulders alone.

As kids, we were pretty good at making up our own rules, but we had nothing on the Pharisees. They took God's laws and layered on rules in an effort to keep people safely distanced from sinning.

The problem with this method was that they were so intent on enforcing the rules, they lost track of the heart of the matter. God hadn't just given rules and commandments to govern His people, but to teach them how to love His way. Imagine how exasperated Jesus as "Lord of the Sabbath" must have been to need to remind the Pharisees that it was in fact good to do good on the Sabbath (Matt. 12:12).

While it is easy to regard the Pharisees with a smirk and eye roll, I think we all, in one way or the other, have been guilty of the same offense.

It can be so easy to get caught up in societal rules which are often selfish (move your feet, lose your seat) and forget that we are called to humility (think of others before ourselves). Our popular rules often glorify a culture that caters to ourselves and shrouds the humility of Heaven.

Jesus spent a lot of time teaching His disciples God's ways over the world's ways. Most of what He said must have sounded a bit crazy:

- Give away my shirt to someone who steals my coat (Matt. 5:40)?
- If someone hits me, turn the other cheek so they can slap that one too (Matt. 5:29)?

Admittingly counter-cultural, these new commands were to teach His followers to live a life that stands out from the world in a culture that valued religion over relationships. Although they may read like just a new list of rules to follow, Jesus's teachings weren't about trading in one list for another.

**Jesus taught how to love each other as His Father loves us.**

Being a Christ follower was never intended to be about upholding rules. It was always about being in right relationship foremost with our Heavenly Father but also with others.

- When religion would shame the man whose hand was lame, Jesus healed him (Matt. 12:9-14).
- When religion forbade association with those "less desirable," Jesus dined with them (Luke 19:1-10).
- When religion called for an eye for an eye, Jesus called His followers to extravagant forgiveness (Matt. 5:38-42).

And, when religion's rules called for blood, Jesus answered, fulfilling all the requirements of the law, He shed His blood so we could live by, in and from love (Matt. 5:17; John 13:34).

Sometimes the "rules" that govern us are ingrained so deeply within that they are hard to recognize. Spend some time in prayer asking God if you are, even unknowingly, governing your life by familial, cultural or religious rules instead of God's love.

If you struggle sometimes, like me, to live from God's love, and find yourself instead living by the rules of our culture and popular society, I challenge you, like Jesus, to be a rule-breaker! Break away from legalistic rules and love others as Jesus did with reckless abandon.

Jesus taught how to love each other as His Father loves us.

# WEEK THIRTY-TWO

*COST*

MATTHEW 13, LUKE 11, 8

MATTHEW 8:14-34, MARK 4-5

MATTHEW 9-10, 14

MARK 6, LUKE 9:1-17, JOHN 6

MATTHEW 15, MARK 7

**MEMORY VERSE**

"WHOEVER TRIES TO KEEP THEIR LIFE WILL LOSE
IT, AND WHOEVER LOSES THEIR LIFE WILL
PRESERVE IT."

**LUKE 17:33**

# LOOSE CHANGE

**BY TAYLOR WATKINS**

My dad has had a change jar on the top of his dresser since I can remember. Nowadays when the jar gets full he dumps it in a Ziplock bag and takes turns giving it to each grandchild. Recently my oldest daughter, Kori, received the change bag. When my dad handed it to her, her eyes gleamed. You could see the wheels turning in her head. Oh the stuffed animal collections she could buy. How many things at the dollar tree could she get? The possibilities were endless in her imaginative little mind.

That Thursday morning she woke up insisting to bring the change to school. Not just the pennies, not just half...the entire bag. Her good news club at school was collecting change for missionaries. They would bring Bibles to people who had never had one before and it would be in their own language.

"I may not be able to buy any toys, but at least I get to help tell people about God." As she spoke those words, my heart melted. To many it may seem like just a bag of change, but to her it was everything she had. She gave it all to share God's word. That day God used my daughter to remind me of the cost of following Jesus.

In Matthew 8, a man is telling Jesus he will follow Him wherever He goes. Well, surely Jesus gave him some comforting words and invited him along for the new journey, right? Not so much. Jesus was not interested in selling people on following Him; He was more of a straight shooter. Jesus replied, "Foxes have dens and birds have nests, but the Son of Man has no place to lay his head" (Matt. 8:20).

Jesus, Messiah, God's one and only Son, homeless. Think of all the places he traveled with dirt lingering on his hands and feet. Imagine the holes in His clothes, stained with sweat and tears. Jesus didn't just tell this man He had to give up his life to follow Him; He taught by example. Jesus gave up everything to do what God called Him to do. People wanted to learn from and be like Jesus, yet they weren't willing to make sacrifices. They wanted Jesus in their life but they didn't want to give their whole life to Jesus. Isn't that like us sometimes?

# "Our God deserves all we have including our 'loose change.'"

If we are honest with ourselves, we may find there is a lot of 'loose change' in our lives we hang onto. We want to spend our time, talents, money, mind, or bodies on things that serve us instead of God. But He wants us to serve Him with everything in our being down to the last brain cell, word, or penny.

He is the one and only Holy God and He is selfish. Not in the way we are selfish. He is selfish because He knows when we give ourselves to anything but Him, we short change ourselves because He is better than anything this world has to offer. **Our God deserves all we have including our "loose change."**

Sister, we are called to dedicate our life to Him. Even if it's all we feel we have left, we give it all to Him for He is worthy.

Do you have some 'loose change' you're holding onto? Where is your mind, body, and soul? Is it aligned with God's glory or your own? Pray and ask the Lord to reveal to you what you are keeping from him and what you need to let go of. Ask Him to help and guide you to give your whole self to Him today, even your "loose change."

# PRAYER GUIDE
*from the Lord's Prayer*

**MATTHEW 6:9-13**

## "THIS, THEN, IS HOW YOU SHOULD PRAY"

As Believers, we know we should pray, but aren't always sure what to pray. Jesus is God, and He's the clearest picture we have of the Father's character and ways. That means when Jesus says to do or not to do something, we should sit up and pay attention.

In Matthew 6:9-13, He told His followers not to pray like the Pharisees, who did it all for show. Then He said, "This, then, is how you should pray" and followed it with the prayer below. Jesus not only taught us how to pray, He modeled a life of prayer for us. The Bible tells us He often withdrew to "lonely places" to commune with God. Today, find a quiet place to steal away for a few minutes, like Jesus, and connect with the Father.

## "OUR FATHER IN HEAVEN"

It is good and right to remember that He is our Lord. But when we come to Him in prayer, the word "Father" reminds us it's not about what we can do for Him— it's about all He does for us. When we come to God in prayer as our personal father, we recognize...

He is approachable.
He knows us personally.
He will provide for us.
We are in need of His care and discipline.

Remembering He is our Father positions our heart in humility and trust.

## "HALLOWED BE YOUR NAME"

Names have meaning. Oftentimes when we read through God's word, we see people's names changed based on the circumstances in their life.
Our God, however, is unchanging. *His name is and will always be Holy.*

God's holiness is what separates Him from us. He is dependent on no one; there is no blemish in Him, "...from him and through him and for him are *all things*..." (Rom 11:36).

Praying "Hallowed be your name" reminds us who we are talking to and that nothing is impossible for Him.

## "YOUR KINGDOM COME"

Have you ever thought about the implications of God being your personal King, and what being a part of God's Kingdom should look like? Jesus taught us to pray, "Your kingdom come," but how does God's Kingdom manifest on earth? Hint: through you and me.

In order to see God's Kingdom come, we must know what His will is, and obediently carry it out. Simply hearing the King's will doesn't accomplish anything— we must put boots on the ground. James 1:22 tells us, "Do not merely listen to the word, and so deceive yourselves. Do what it says." Praying "Your Kingdom come" reminds us to ask, "God, what is my part in furthering your Kingdom today?"

## "YOUR WILL BE DONE ON EARTH AS IT IS IN HEAVEN"

We don't have to wonder what God's will is for our family, our job, our marriage and our finances— He's already made it known. His desire is that, in every circumstance, we will be transformed, more and more, into His image. When I'm anxious and tempted to enforce my own will on God, I remind myself of two things: First, God loves me and always has my best interest at heart— that is my transformation into His image, body, soul, and spirit. Second, while I see things from a limited perspective, God sees things in the light of eternity.

Praying, "your will be done" reminds us that God sees the big picture when we don't. We can trust His will because He loves us. What is one thing that you are struggling or worrying about today that you can give over to God and trust His will to be done?

## "GIVE US TODAY OUR DAILY BREAD"

I love that Jesus taught us to pray, "Give us today our daily bread." Saying that simple statement out loud reminds me of a few things— First, that God *freely gives*. I don't have to work or beg for this bread. I simply need to receive it. Second, I must show up *today and every* day to the table. I can't listen to a good sermon once a week and expect it to sustain me. Like the manna in the desert, Jesus desires for us to seek Him anew every morning. Last, but not least, Jesus is *enough*. He not only meets— *He exceeds*— every spiritual need I have. He nurtures and sustains me. He is all-sufficient.

What do you need from God today? Love? Grace? Strength? Joy? Assurance? Praying "give us today our daily bread" reminds us that He will readily and abundantly supply.

## "FORGIVE US OUR DEBTS, AS WE ALSO HAVE FORGIVEN OUR DEBTORS"

This part of the Lord's prayer prompts me to lay my life out before God in examination— if God forgave me the way I currently forgive others, to what extent would that be? Often I don't like the answer to that question.

I don't know about you, but sometimes I try to give God excuses for why I shouldn't have to forgive a certain person who caused hurt. If you've never done this, spoiler alert: those excuses don't hold up in God's court. Jesus had every reason to give up on us, to say, "that's enough," yet He didn't. In His final breath He called out to God on our behalf, for our forgiveness. Praying "forgive us our debts, as we also have forgiven our debtors" reminds us to forgive others in the same way we need forgiven.

## "LEAD US NOT INTO TEMPTATION, BUT DELIVER US FROM EVIL"

When I pray this part of the Lord's prayer, it reminds me of something important: my human predisposition to be led astray into sin. Too often I let my guard down, thinking I've "overcome" a particular sin or addiction. It's in those moments of pride that I'm ripe for Satan's picking.

Praying "lead me not into temptation" keeps me humbly reliant on God's counsel. Humility is key to victory. When we pray this prayer, we give God permission to convict our hearts before we even entertain the idea of acting on a sinful desire.

## "FOR YOURS IS THE KINGDOM"

Can you imagine if we ruled over God's Kingdom? It would be a total disaster. We are terrible at running our own lives. When we decide to reign over ourselves, instead of following the Spirit, it only leads to destruction. Praying the words, "For yours is the Kingdom," helps us acknowledge who holds ownership over it: the Lord. It reminds us why we do what we do as Christians: Love God, love people, and lead people to Him. Not for our glory, but for His.

God's Word tells us the kingdoms of this earth will all pass away— that includes yours and mine. But God's Kingdom will reign forever. Praying "yours is the Kingdom" invites us to turn our focus from our kingdoms to God's Kingdom today, knowing the impact is everlasting.

## "YOURS IS THE POWER"

The truth is, we don't have the power within us to walk out this life God has called us to live. Here's the good news: He does. *And His power is unlimited.* I spent many years striving to be the perfect Jesus-follower and it only led to burnout. It wasn't until I plugged into the Source that I discovered the freedom in His power working through me to accomplish His will. Now, when I pray, "Yours is the power," I like to add, *"not mine."*

How do we access God's power? *"We have received all of this by coming to know him" (2 Peter 1:3, NLT).* There is power in His presence, friend. When we know Him through His Word, and through prayer, we experience His power and it is manifested in us. Praying "yours is the power" reminds us to draw near, plug in, and receive from His unlimited source today.

## "YOURS IS THE GLORY"

Have you ever noticed that people or teams who idolize themselves often self-destruct? The Bible calls them fools because they poison themselves with their own ways instead of drinking the living water that comes from God alone.

The successes we have on this earth, big or small, are achieved through the same power that raised Jesus Christ from the dead. It is not us, but the Spirit living inside us that makes all things come together for good. He equips regular people, like you and me, to fulfill His plans for His purpose and ultimate glory. God is the hero. Not us. Praying, "yours is the Glory" helps us to take our eyes off of ourselves, so that we may recognize His hand in every waking moment and give Him the praise.

## "AMEN"

We end our prayers with "Amen," but have you ever stopped to think about what that means? It means "truly," or "let it be." God hears us, and when we pray according to His will, we will have what we ask of Him. Here's the good news: the Lord's prayer is clearly the Lord's will. That means when we pray it with sincere hearts we have a 100% chance He will respond. It may not look like what we think it will (it often doesn't), but rest assured: He is good and faithful.

As you begin to incorporate the Lord's Prayer into your everyday life, don't forget the deeply powerful meaning of that simple last word, "Amen"— truly, we have what we ask of Him.

*Excerpts taken from our "Kingdom Focus: 10 Days of Prayer & Fasting" guide, available for free at*
*www.rootedmoms.com/resources*

*I am praying for...*

_____
_____
_____
_____
_____
_____
_____
_____
_____
_____
_____
_____
_____

Note: For this prayer guide, we utilized the NIV translation of the Lord's Prayer. The final portion ("For yours is the kingdom and the power and the glory forever. Amen.") is not included in all manuscripts, however we chose to include it for the purpose of our study.

# WEEK THIRTY-THREE

## KNOW

MATTHEW 16, MARK 8, LUKE 9:18-27

MATTHEW 17, MARK 9, LUKE 9:28-62

MATTHEW 18, JOHN 7-8

JOHN 9-10:21, LUKE 10

JOHN 10:22-42, LUKE 12

## MEMORY VERSE

"BUT GROW IN THE GRACE AND KNOWLEDGE OF OUR LORD AND SAVIOR JESUS CHRIST. TO HIM BE GLORY BOTH NOW AND FOREVER! AMEN."

**2 PETER 3:18**

# GETTING TO KNOW JESUS

**BY JESSICA PARKER**

My husband and I met late one May while we were both on summer break from college. We spent those summer months getting to know each other before we both went back to school, four hours away from one other.

We both knew early on that we wanted to stay together despite the distance. For the next two years we spent our days getting to know each other through text, phone calls, and my favorite, old school hand-written letters through the mail! We were intentional about the time we spent together and the conversations we had when we were apart.

In July 2012, we got married and started our life together. All those conversations and time spent together over those two years definitely helped us get to know each other. However, nothing compares to the knowledge you gain waking up, and doing life next to someone day in and day out.

Truly knowing someone takes time and intention; it doesn't happen overnight with the snap of a finger. We experience this not only in our marriages but also in our everyday lives.

I don't meet someone on the street and instantly know their whole story and what makes them the person they are. However, when I was younger, I thought because I went to church every Sunday, I knew everything there was to know about Jesus. But here I am at 32 still learning new things about Him everyday.

For that, I am so grateful and it never ceases to amaze me when God reveals something new to me.

In Mark 9, we see Jesus and his disciples leave where they were. Verse 30 says, "Jesus did not want anyone to know where they were because he was teaching his disciples." Jesus took the time to train his disciples in depth. He spent intentional time with them and they with Him.

Deep spiritual growth isn't instant, regardless of the quality of experience or teaching. The disciples lived, ate and traveled with Jesus every day. If they needed to lay everything aside periodically in order to learn from the Master, how much more do we need to set aside time to spend with God to get to know Him better?

As I write this, my husband and I have been married almost ten years. In order for us to have a healthy marriage, we have to continue being intentional about pouring into our relationship and spending time together. The same is true of our relationship with Christ. No matter where we are in our spiritual journey, no matter how mature we are in our faith, we still have room for growth.

Friend, if you want to know more about Jesus, find a way to draw closer to Him today. For you, maybe that is reading a chapter in Proverbs, listening to a new worship song in the car, or spending an extra five minutes in prayer today. **To know Jesus better, return to Him day after day.**

He will continue to meet you and align your spirit with His truth. Rest in the comfort of knowing that the longer you walk with him, the better you will understand who He is. Ask Him to meet you where you are and reveal more of himself to you.

"To know Jesus better, return to Him day after day."

# WEEK THIRTY-FOUR

## COMFORT

LUKE 13-15

LUKE 16, JOHN 11, LUKE 17

LUKE 18:1-14, MARK 10, MATTHEW 19

MATTHEW 20-21, LUKE 18:15-43

LUKE 19, MARK 11

## MEMORY VERSE

"PRAISE BE TO THE GOD AND FATHER OF OUR LORD JESUS CHRIST, THE FATHER OF COMPASSION AND THE GOD OF ALL COMFORT, WHO COMFORTS US IN ALL OUR TROUBLES, SO THAT WE CAN COMFORT THOSE IN ANY TROUBLE WITH THE COMFORT WE OURSELVES RECEIVE FROM GOD."

2 CORINTHIANS 1:3-4

# CHOOSING GRIEF

**BY WENDY GERDES**

Sitting in the coffee shop with my friend, the tears flowed. I sat in the chair in the corner of the small room clasping my hands tightly around my coffee cup trying to chase away the feeling of empty arms. The air hurt my lungs and the emptiness inside threatened to overtake me. Days felt like nightmares and sleep was relief because in my dreams, our little girl was still tucked safely inside. The recent memories of the silent delivery and holding her lifeless form in a tiny white dress haunted my waking moments. Grief was the air I breathed and I did not know if the air would ever clear again.

And there she sat and kept sitting. My friend sat with me in my space of grief. She wasn't afraid but allowed herself to feel my pain. Her tears flowed too, healing my heart one tear at a time. Her tears puddled with mine and the grief lifted a bit from me as she took some of it on herself. I wasn't alone, but I had a friend who was with me. She didn't allow me to suffer alone. She didn't stand outside my grief and talk to me from without, but came near enough to allow the rawness to touch her. She cried; she wondered; she listened and she sat. She was like a shadow on a sunny day. She kept showing up. She was fiercely persistent.

In our grief, we remember the ones who show up. Jesus shows us how to be one who does.

In John 11, there is a story I have always been fascinated by. Jesus' good friend Lazarus died and friends and family were grief-stricken. The One who raised the dead had a close friend who died. No wonder Mary and Martha, Lazarus's sisters, were perplexed. Surely Jesus could have prevented the heartache. Had He come earlier, there would have been no grief, no tears and no funeral. He could have just showed up, marched up to that closed up tomb and called Lazarus out, but that's not what He did.

First, He allowed grief to touch Him and then John 11:35 says, "Jesus *wept*" (emphasis added). He chose to feel the grief. He took a moment to sit in their space and feel what they felt. He felt the pain and allowed Himself to be moved by it. There is profound power when grief is shared by another. **Entering another's grief allows us to partner with God to bring healing to a hurting heart.**

> "Entering another's grief allows us to partner with God to bring healing to a hurting heart."

Jesus was the exact representation of who God is and the story of Lazarus reveals God's heart towards us. God comes to us with compassion in our hard spaces. He doesn't watch us from afar, but comes near. He is not distant, but sits with us in our difficult moments.

He is not unfeeling or uncaring, but chooses to feel deeply when we are in pain. He is not a God who does not allow emotion to touch Him but voluntarily moves into those places with us. We can come to Him no matter what it is we are carrying and be sure of His tender compassion and care. We are never alone. He is with us. Sometimes He comes near us through another, just as my friend did for me.

We, too, can learn to be near others as Jesus was. We can choose to enter into other's places of grief and offer our tears. Through shared tears, healing eventually comes.

# 35

## WEEK
## THIRTY-FIVE

*GREATNESS*

MARK 12, JOHN 12, MATTHEW 22

MATTHEW 23, LUKE 20-21

MARK 13, MATTHEW 24-25

MATTHEW 26, MARK 14, LUKE 22

JOHN 13-14

**MEMORY VERSE**

"EVEN AS THE SON OF MAN DID NOT COME TO BE
SERVED, BUT TO SERVE, AND TO GIVE HIS LIFE AS
A RANSOM FOR MANY."

**MATTHEW 20:28**

# THE G.O.A.T.

**BY TIERNEY NASHLEANAS**

The night light in the nursery cast a faint warm glow across the walls; the room was clean, calm and perfectly decorated. I was supposed to take my precious newborn babe, swaddle him just so, feed him, turn on the sound machine, sing a song, place him in the crib and walk away to the sound of silence, just like the books said to do. He cried. I cried.

My desire to be great had grown and given birth in my heart long before my son's birth made me a mama. The clinking of the metals on my letter jacket as I walked down the hall in my high school fulfilled my desire for status. The applause of the crowd after a performance in a notable venue made me feel as if all the effort was noticed and worthy of much praise. The glowing reviews at work on my job performance reinforced the image of my own greatness that I was trying to project.

I would have (and still do) fit in with the scribes, Pharisees and even the disciples.

The scribes and Pharisees wanted to be noticed, honored and praised for their knowledge of the Torah and interpretation of the Law of Moses. Their traditions became so over the top that they were described in Matthew 23:4 by Jesus as laying heavy burdens on people's shoulders that were hard to bear. Jesus also talked about how, "They do all their deeds to be seen by others...[and]... love the place of honor at feasts and the best seats in the synagogues" (Matt. 23:5-6). They wanted their names to be made known above all and their obsession for standing, status and self-indulgence became a presence of oppression.

Jesus warned against their ways and provided an opposite alternative to greatness during the last supper. As the disciples sat with Jesus, they began to argue about who was the greatest among them. It appears that even they were not immune to the allure of status, honor and power the world had to offer.

Jesus demonstrated true humility and taught them that greater is the one who serves rather than the one that is served (Luke 22:26). Then as an act of love for his disciples, he gets up from the table and prepares to wash their feet (John 13: 4-5).

> "The cure for self-concern is to focus on Christ's greatness rather than our own."

Jesus humbled himself to the status of servant as He removed his outer garments, poured water in the basin, kneeled and washed the miles of filth off of his disciples feet. The highest became the lowest and the master became the servant. Their eyes were opened to the greatness of God as Jesus fulfilled their need for love and forgiveness through a humble act of service.

**The cure for self-concern is to focus on Christ's greatness rather than our own.**

When are you tempted by the allure of status, honor and power? Like me, do you try to establish your own greatness through parenting outcomes, job performance and accomplishments? Does it feel like your desire for greatness becomes a weight too heavy to bear?

Dear friend, Jesus loves you. He died on the cross and bore the weight of your self-serving sin, and mine, so that we could be free from the pressures of this world. Unlike our wants and desires that we so desperately pursue, Jesus is near; He is attainable and He wants to work in and through you.

When you notice your motives are self-serving, cry out to God saying, "Lord, will you please open my eyes to the ways in which I have sought my own greatness instead of yours. I thank you that I am forgiven for these things because of your death on the cross and victory over sin. Give me a heart to see the pain of others and enter into it with humility and love so that I may serve them, just like you serve me. Amen."

# WEEK THIRTY-FIVE
## TAKEAWAY

# 36

## WEEK
## THIRTY-SIX

### RESPONSE

JOHN 15-17

LUKE 23, MARK 15, MATTHEW 27

MATTHEW 28, JOHN 18-19

MARK 16, LUKE 24

JOHN 20-21

**MEMORY VERSE**

"REPENT AND BE BAPTIZED, EVERY ONE OF YOU,
IN THE NAME OF JESUS CHRIST FOR THE
FORGIVENESS OF YOUR SINS. AND YOU WILL
RECEIVE THE GIFT OF THE HOLY SPIRIT."

**ACTS 2:38**

# WHAT'S YOUR RESPONSE?

**BY HEATHER KENNY**

It's an election year here in Belize. Our government is structured similar to Canada or New Zealand. We are led by a prime minister and two houses of legislation - a senate composed of members appointed by the current government, and a house of representatives elected from the six districts in Belize. As a permanent resident but not a citizen, I do not have the right to vote here, but I still try to understand the political system.

As in any political climate, the responses from the Belizean people are varied. Some believe the current political party is the answer to all of the country's hardships. Others believe this party will bring nothing but destruction to the people and economy. The same is true for the opposing party. Some tolerate the current leadership; others vocally oppose it. There is no end to the varied responses to change brought about by those in authority.

To say that Jesus brought change into the world is an understatement. He wasn't what people expected, yet He fulfilled over 300 prophecies from the Old Testament. The Gospels record various responses that people had to Jesus:

- The high priests and religious leaders were jealous and plotted His death (Matt. 27:1-2)
- Judas betrayed Him (John 18:2-6)
- Pilate washed his hands of Him (Matt. 27:24)
- The crowd praised Him and then called for His crucifixion (Mark 11:8-10; Matt 27: 22-23)
- Soldiers mocked Him (Mark 15:16-20)
- Simon from Cyrene has his life interrupted by Him (Mark 15:21)
- Criminals on the cross insulted Him (Matt. 27:44)
- One criminal on the cross believed in Him (Luke 23:42)
- The captain of the guard recognized Him as the Son of God (Mark 15:39)
- Joseph of Arimathea honored Him (Luke 23:50-54)
- Mary and the women followed Him (John 19:25)
- Herod saw Him as a spectacle and wanted to be entertained by Him (Luke 23:8-10)
- Two men on the road to Emmaus failed to recognize Him (Luke 24:13-32)
- Thomas doubted Him (John 20:24-25)
- Peter denied Him (John 18:27)
- The High Priest interrogated Him (John 18:19)

- Nicodemus revered Him (John 19:39)
- The disciples acknowledged Him (John 21:7)

Today, almost 2,000 years later, people still respond to Jesus in a multitude of different ways. You, friend, have a choice of how you will respond to Him, too.

Here's the amazing part.

**Jesus has only ever had ONE response to us: love and forgiveness.**

No matter how many ways we see ourselves and those around us responding to Jesus, He never wavers. He only sees us through eyes of perfect love. He unendingly offers forgiveness.

How have you found yourself responding to Jesus? Have you washed your hands of Him like Pilate did? Have you insulted Him like the criminals on the cross? Maybe you've found yourself praising Him one day and cursing Him the next, like the crowd did.

Whatever your past responses may have been, it is your response to Him today that matters. Accept His love and forgiveness with a humble, "Thank you, Jesus!"

"Jesus has only ever had ONE response to us: love and forgiveness."

# R.O.O.T.

## JOURNALING GUIDE

It's one thing to read God's Word; it's another thing to actually *understand* and *apply* it.

Move from information to practical application with our tried-and-true R.O.O.T. study method. Use your journal to walk through the following steps for each day's reading:

### READ

Read the passage of Scripture, highlighting or underlining any words or phrases that stick out to you.

### OWN WORDS

Shorten the overall story or message into your own words.

### OBSERVE

Jot down your observations. Here are some questions to get you started—
- Who is the author of this book/letter and what do we know about them?
- To whom was this book/letter written?
- What is the central theme of today's passage?
- What words or phrases stick out to you the most and why?
- Does any part reference or remind you of an Old Testament story or something Jesus taught?
- Were there any statements that rubbed you the wrong way or confused you?*

### TAKEAWAY

Think about today's passages—
- What is one step you can take to live more like Jesus, in light of the truth(s) you learned today?
- How does this passage encourage you and strengthen your faith?

*We love the Enduring Word Commentary for all those hard-to-understand moments in Scripture! Visit www.enduringword.com or download the app for quick and easy access.*

# WEEK THIRTY-SEVEN

37

## AUTHOR

ACTS 1-2

ACTS 3-4

ACTS 5-6

ACTS 7-8

ACTS 9-10

## MEMORY VERSE

"'FOR MY THOUGHTS ARE NOT YOUR THOUGHTS, NEITHER ARE YOUR WAYS MY WAYS,' DECLARES THE LORD. 'AS FAR AS THE HEAVENS ARE HIGHER THAN THE EARTH, SO ARE MY WAYS HIGHER THAN YOUR WAYS AND MY THOUGHTS THAN YOUR THOUGHTS.'"

**ISAIAH 55:8-9**

# TRUSTING THE AUTHOR

**BY KRISTEN WILLIAMSON**

When my son was 11 months old, my husband and I decided to try for another baby. Just one month after we started trying, we were blessed with that big, fat positive! We bought "big brother" clothes, started telling family, and dreaming of everything to come.

Then, while my father-in-law was visiting, I started having immense pain and other miscarriage symptoms. My husband and I decided I should go to the ER where we were informed we lost our sweet baby, Riley. I remember exactly how every piece of that night played out. I especially remember the big question I had for God: *why?*

Whether you've experienced a miscarriage or another tragedy, you may have had this same question swirling around in your head keeping you awake at night, interrupting the joyous moments in life, pulling you away from God.

In the book of Acts, written by Luke, we learn some of the history of the early church. There is a Greek word that we see 22 times in the Book of Acts and that word is "dei." "Dei" is translated as "it is necessary".* Which means that Luke is driving home the point that things are necessary throughout history because it is in God's plan. In the very first chapter of the book, Luke hits us with the hard truth: "it is not for you to know times or seasons that the Father has fixed by his own authority" (Acts 1:7).

We see some amazing works done by God in the first ten chapters of the Book of Acts:
- Peter and John are used by God to heal a lame man (Acts 3).
- Stephen performs work and wonders to build faith amongst people (Acts 7), and
- Peter falls into a trance as God directs him to not call any person unclean (Acts 10).

A commonality can be found amongst all these things, God is in control even when He is working through people. Knowing all this gave me confidence in two things: 1) I do not get to know the why for everything that happens, and 2) God is still in control.

It can be hard to fully trust that God is in control when things feel uncertain, messy, and painful. We live in a broken world. As humans, we often feel like we need to know who, what, when, where, and why to be confident that things are going smoothly and there's no need for panic. However, Jeremiah 17:7 tells us, "...blessed is the one who trusts in the Lord, whose confidence is in him."

So I ask, what matters more, knowing everything and constantly worrying when things don't go according to your plan? Or being blessed greatly and trusting in God's most perfect plan for you?

Sweet friend, God is in control always. Jesus dying on the cross? He knew. Christians being persecuted? He knew. **God is sovereign through it all.** Luke gives us a glimpse of this truth stating, "this Jesus, delivered up according to the definite plan and foreknowledge of God" (Acts 2:23). While there were many sins committed around the crucifixion of Jesus, God's plan was always to send His son down to die on the cross for our sins. His perfect plan was still brought to completion even amidst the brokenness of the world.

So the next time a door closes, take a moment to thank God for always being with you. For creating a most perfect plan for you that might not be what you envisioned but will bear so much fruit to you and those around you.

"God is sovereign through it all."

*Strong, James. "The Exhaustive Concordance of the Bible." Hendrickson Publication, 2021.
https://biblehub.com/greek/1163.htm

# WEEK
# THIRTY-EIGHT

## 38

### ACTION

ACTS 11-12

ACTS 13-14

JAMES 1-2

JAMES 3-4

JAMES 5

**MEMORY VERSE**

"DO NOT MERELY LISTEN TO THE WORD, AND SO DECEIVE YOURSELVES. DO WHAT IT SAYS."

**JAMES 1:22**

# FAITH AND ACTION

**BY DEBBIE BURNS**

Hurricane Katrina brought devastation to the Mississippi coastline where I lived with my family in August 2005. Many lost their lives; twelve bodies washed up just two blocks from our home. We were without power and water for a few weeks. Military helicopters dropped MRE's in our neighborhood and attempts at preparing warm meals were cooked over sterno.

After a few weeks, my family had power and water again. We were truly thankful, but aware that many were still without power, water, shelter, and hope. It was important to share my faith in some tangible way to these hurting people. I asked God what I could do. His answer was clear, "Bake chocolate chip cookies." So I did.

The message, with smiley faces I taped to each bag of chocolate chip cookies, was simple. It stated that the little bag of cookies was a reminder that Jesus loves them along with this verse, "...the joy of the Lord is your strength" (Neh. 8:10). I included our names and phone number for prayer. My husband and teenage son passed out dozens of bags to people standing in the lines for assistance all over our city.

A few weeks later this message was on our home answering machine, "I found a bag with your phone number on the floor of a hotel here in New Orleans. I checked into this hotel to commit suicide. I had forgotten that Jesus loved me until I read the message on your bag. I am going to find Jesus again and go on with life, but I wouldn't have if I hadn't found your message. I just want to thank you."

In James chapter 2, the connection between faith and actions is clear. James mentioned that both Abraham and Rahab were considered righteous by God because of their faith and actions. Abraham's faith and actions worked together when he willingly brought his son Isaac to the altar, "His actions made his faith complete" (Jas. 2:22). Rahab's faith and actions worked together when she hid the Israelite spies in Jericho (Jas. 2:25).

The results of the faith and actions of Abraham and Rahab were amazing, too. Not only did Abraham become the father of the entire Jewish people, but he was also considered a friend of God. Not only was Rahab and her entire household saved when the walls of Jericho fell, but she was mentioned in the lineage of Jesus Christ in Matthew 1:5.

Faith and action work together as James explains, "You see that a person is considered righteous by what they do and not by faith alone" (Jas. 2:24). **True faith ignites a passion for action.**

Those actions are the fruit of our faith. I consider my act of faith small when compared to the size of the need by the hurricane victims, but it was done for God's glory. God is the one who orchestrated the amazing result. Honestly we may never see the results of acting on our faith, but that does not mean the results were any less amazing.

Let your faith ignite your passion for action. Acting on my faith had an amazing result. Do what God drops into your heart to do. It could be as big as starting a business or moving to another country as a missionary. It could be unimpressively ordinary like stopping to talk to someone who crosses your path. It could be helpful like babysitting or planting flowers. It could be baking chocolate chip cookies.

No action that is done for God's glory is too small. After all, faith as small as a mustard seed can move mountains (Matt. 17:20)!

# WEEK THIRTY-NINE

## YIELD

ACTS 15-16

GALATIANS 1-2

GALATIANS 3-4

GALATIANS 5-6

ACTS 17-18

**MEMORY VERSE**

"IT IS FOR FREEDOM THAT CHRIST HAS SET US FREE.
STAND FIRM, THEN, AND DO NOT LET YOURSELVES
BE BURDENED AGAIN BY A YOKE OF SLAVERY."

**GALATIANS 5:1**

# YIELDING TO YIELD

**BY LONETTE M. BAITY**

I've just come back from an amazing women's retreat where I've seen Jesus do the miraculous. For three days, our team seemed to live in the book of Acts. We went where we felt the Holy Spirit prompted us. We said what we felt He wanted us to say and when we felt Him pause, we stopped in our tracks.

The entire experience was invigorating. My heart was full and I've spent the past week trying to savor every last moment of standing on holy ground where the Spirit of Jesus seems to flow so freely.

"This must be it," I've said to myself. "This is living by the Spirit. And I have to [insert checklist here] in order to maintain this sacred space." As soon as I started to place pressure on myself to do "the things," the harder it became to stick to all the guidelines I set for myself. Can you relate?

Don't get me wrong! I believe spiritual disciplines help us connect with God and grow in maturity. Oddly enough as I read our passages for this week, I find living in a sacred space and walking by the Spirit is so much deeper and yet, much simpler than I could ever maintain on my own.

In Galatians, Paul cautions Gentile believers about getting bogged down by Jewish law. They had been saved by their faith in Jesus as Messiah. Now, they were allowing themselves to be confused and trapped by others' ideas of what it would take to maintain their salvation and grow. Paul reminds his readers to stand firm in the freedom that comes from God's grace (Gal. 5:1).

In a nutshell, Paul teaches us: **In order to yield the fruit of the Holy Spirit in our lives, we must yield to the Holy Spirit!**

The Holy Spirit - not rule-following or checklist-checking - maintains the ground of hearts in order to produce good fruit. That fruit may or may not include miracles, signs and wonders on a daily basis. (This feels like a bummer for me).

The fruit the Spirit produces is seen in the daily grind and grit of toilet scrubbing. Where childrearing gets rough and where preteen attitudes abound, patience and kindness can be found in a life yielded to the Holy Spirit. Our roots can go down deep into the sacred ground and we can soak up water from the Living well. The Spirit of Jesus within us makes this possible. When we walk close enough to step in rhythm with His heartbeat, near enough to hear His whisper, we can't help but produce His fruit.

Oh, how my heart longs to truly live this way - free from the rules and checklists, simply saying, "Yes!" to the Holy Spirit. If you feel the same way, consider doing a heart check today. What is one area you are yielding fruit? What is one area you can yield more fully to the work of the Holy Spirit?

"In order to yield the fruit of the Holy Spirit in our lives, we must yield to the Holy Spirit!"

# WEEK FORTY

### *SIMPLICITY*

1 THESSALONIANS 1-3

1 THESSALONIANS 4-5

2 THESSALONIANS 1-2

2 THESSALONIANS 3, ACTS 19

1 CORINTHIANS 1-2

## MEMORY VERSE

"WE ARE THEREFORE CHRIST'S AMBASSADORS, AS
THOUGH GOD WERE MAKING HIS APPEAL THROUGH
US. WE IMPLORE YOU ON CHRIST'S BEHALF: BE
RECONCILED TO GOD."

**2 CORINTHIANS 5:20**

# THE SECRET OF SIMPLE

**BY RENEE ROBINSON**

A little boy walked into the room carrying a video camera. I watched him setting up various shots, quietly concentrating on his work. He informed me he wanted to grow up to be a YouTube star. The boy had a message to share with the world.

We now have endless opportunities to share our messages with the world. You simply have to become a master at grabbing people's attention and holding it over all the competition on the internet. There's a pressure to be funnier, more clever, more spectacular, louder, more insightful, bolder, or more extreme than the others.

The latest trend with Instagram reels has me captivated. Its effect is hypnotizing as I watch someone point to bubbles while music plays. I may not remember what they shared, but I will remember their entertaining tactics. For all the hard work, it can be distracting to the message.

In 1 Corinthians chapter 2, Paul proclaims he did not use tactics to gain the attention of his hearers. He came with no persuasive words, no brilliant speech, no pizazz of any kind. It wasn't because he couldn't; rather, it was because his message was so powerful he dared not hinder it by getting in the way:

"And so it was with me, brothers and sisters. When I came to you, I did not come with eloquence or human wisdom as I proclaimed to you the testimony about God. For resolved to know nothing while I was with you except Jesus Christ and him crucified. I came to you in weakness with great fear and trembling. My message and my preaching were not with wise and persuasive words, but with a demonstration of the Spirit's power, so that your faith might not rest on human wisdom, but on God's power." 1 Corinthians 2:1-5

Paul was known for his oratory skills. He was powerfully persuasive. But he didn't want people to be drawn to him because of his ability to wow them with his words. Paul wanted to make men followers of Jesus by the power of the Spirit rather than the giftedness of Paul.

"With the gospel, the power is in the message not the deliverer or delivery."

**With the gospel, the power is in the message not the deliverer or delivery.**

The secret is in simplicity. Simple leaves room for the message to marinate in the hearts of the hearers. The simple message and truth allows space to think and respond.

Each of us carries the message of the gospel everywhere we go. We are all ambassadors for Christ, sent to tell the world of His good news (2 Cor. 5:20).

Do you feel ill-equipped to share the good news of Jesus? Maybe you see the endless creativity online when others share their messages. You have a message to share, too, but it can feel daunting when we feel we have to resort to creative tactics to draw people in. Remember Paul's example; he carried the simple gospel so as not to distract. We can rest in the simple gospel knowing it's all we need to share the good news of Jesus. A simple message faithfully shared is better than an eloquent speech never delivered.

Remember the acronym KISS: Keep it simple, sweetie.

Christ, in and through us, will spread a pleasing aroma and draw people toward us (2 Cor. 2:14-15). They will be ready to hear the good news we have to share because they will want to know the secret for the joy inside. Remember Christ is working in and through you; all you have to do is spread His sweet aroma and share the simple, powerful message of the cross.

# WEEK FORTY-ONE

## VESSEL

1 CORINTHIANS 3-4

1 CORINTHIANS 5-6

1 CORINTHIANS 7-8

1 CORINTHIANS 9-10

1 CORINTHIANS 11-12

## MEMORY VERSE

"SO NEITHER THE ONE WHO PLANTS NOR THE ONE WHO WATERS IS ANYTHING, BUT ONLY GOD, WHO MAKES THINGS GROW."

1 CORINTHIANS 3:7

# YOU PLANT, GOD GROWS

**BY JANNETTA COX**

When I was sixteen, my life forever changed. While I grew up in church, it wasn't until that moment at a youth conference where I felt the love and presence of God more than I ever had before. At the conference, I realized I wanted my generation, and generations to come, to know God in the same way that I was getting to know Him. Years later, I began to serve as a youth leader at my local church. I loved teaching, mentoring, and praying that each student would know God at an early age just as I did. Focusing all my time and energy on the students, I would lead small groups, teach the word, counsel them, and be readily available to them via text/phone. What I didn't realize was that burnout was lurking around the corner.

Desperately (and frustratingly), I attempted to keep each student on the straight and narrow. At the same time, I was also trying to be their mentor, counselor, and friend. The students looked to me for everything and to be honest, it made me feel special. When the burnout set in, I could no longer sustain it and had to step back from doing what I once loved. By looking back, I recognize that the burnout stemmed from pointing the students to myself as their leader when I should have been pointing them to Christ.

In my struggle to find my place as leader, I wish I took a deeper dive into this week's reading. In 1 Corinthians, we find the Corinthian church struggling with a series of issues from division to sexual immorality. Paul, being the spiritual father and leader he was to the Corinthians, found it imperative to write a letter warning them. One thing he addressed was how leaders should be viewed within the church. At the time, the Corinthians exalted Paul and Apollos as their leaders. So much so, that it caused division between them. They would pride themselves on who they were most loyal to. In 1 Corinthians 3:4, we see some would boastfully profess, "I follow Paul" while others would proudly declare, "I follow Apollos."

Paul did not take pride in them fighting in such a way. He recognized that without God he and Apollos were nothing. In 1 Corinthians 3:5, Paul states, "What, after all, is Apollos? And what is Paul? Only servants, through whom you came to believe—as the Lord has assigned to each his task." He made it very clear that he and Apollos were merely vessels used by God. He further reiterated this by using a planting metaphor.

"Our purpose in everything we do is to point the lost and hurting back to Jesus, and Jesus alone."

While Paul planted the seed of the gospel and Apollos watered it, it is only through God that there is growth. In 1 Corinthians 3:7 Paul continues by saying, "so neither the one who plants nor the one who waters is anything, but only God who makes things grow." Paul's response to the Corinthians is humbling and unfortunately lost on society today. It is so easy to exalt others and oneself in the name of God. Social media has only highlighted this issue further. How often is it that we see pastors or Bible teachers with multitudes of followers hanging on to their every word? Instead of looking to God's word in times of trouble, we find ourselves looking to our favorite pastor.

Not only do we see this on social media, but we can also see this in our very own lives. Has there ever been a time where you desperately wanted to lead someone to Christ, but found yourself leading in your own strength or capacity? Have you ever found yourself leading from a place of your own selfish ambition? While serving others is a wonderful thing, we must not forget our purpose in it all. **Our purpose in everything we do is to point the lost and hurting back to Jesus, and Jesus alone.**

What does this look like? Now as I serve, my prayer specifically is, "God thank you for giving me the ability to be a vessel used by you. As I serve, help me be obedient to you alone. I ask that you go before me, giving me the words to say and the steps to take as I serve my brothers and sisters in Christ." I also examine my motives. Am I acting in obedience to God, or my own selfish ambition?

When searching for answers, are you looking to God or your favorite Bible teacher? More importantly, when leading others are you pointing them to Christ or yourself? Like Paul, let us humble ourselves by realizing that neither we nor our favorite pastor is God. We never can be. However, He has given us the wonderful privilege as believers to be used by Him for His good works!

# 42

## WEEK FORTY-TWO

### LABOR

1 CORINTHIANS 13-14

1 CORINTHIANS 15-16

2 CORINTHIANS 1-2

2 CORINTHIANS 3-4

2 CORINTHIANS 5-6

## MEMORY VERSE

"LOVE DOES NOT DELIGHT IN EVIL BUT REJOICES WITH THE TRUTH. IT ALWAYS PROTECTS, ALWAYS TRUSTS, ALWAYS HOPES, AND ALWAYS PERSEVERES."

**1 CORINTHIANS 13:6-7**

# LABOR OF LOVE

**BY AUDRA POWERS**

I will never forget taking my first pregnancy test on July 4th. My husband and I were on our way back from a mini road trip to celebrate the holiday weekend. I had a feeling that would be one of our last solo trips together. Two pink lines-I knew it! He cried; I laughed. We were thrilled. At my first doctor's appointment I enrolled in the hospital's new mom program called Labor of Love. The nurse sent me home with a huge information packet on all things labor and delivery. We read all the books, made all the lists, purchased all the things, and then there was the actual "bringing home baby" part no one could ever prepare us for!

Fast forward five years and two more bundles of joy later, we are now a family of five. And let me tell you, there has been a lot of strenuous labor raising three little ones. Wasn't labor and delivery supposed to be the hard part?! Parenting is truly a labor of love.

1 Corinthians 13 is the famous love chapter in the Bible. In verse five we read that love is patient, kind, does not envy, or boast. But if we keep reading into verse six and seven, we notice more characteristics of love. In Charles Spurgeon's sermon titled "Love's Labours," he notes that there are four labors of love: love bears all things, believes all things, hopes all things, and endures all things. In verse seven, we read that 'Love always protects, always trusts, always hopes, and always perseveres." These characteristics give us tangible ways to love the ones around us.

I remember the intense feeling of love when I held my baby for the first time. I also remember the pregnancy pains, non-stop nursing sessions, caring for my colicky infant, potty training, toddler tantrums, terrible twos, and all the work that goes into taking care of my children each day-the labors of love. After reading the passages in 1 Corinthians it made me stop and think. I labor all day long in taking care of my children's needs, but do I labor well? Do I labor in love?

At first glance I would tally up my imperfections and say, "No." I don't feel like I labor in love most days. I lose my temper. I feel frustrated with the limitations of my little ones. And there are days that I feel like I've failed. Maybe I was too distracted by my phone to join in a game of cards, or maybe I yelled out of frustration. There are plenty of examples I can come up with when I didn't respond to my family with love.

I will never be a perfect mother, but I do have a perfect Heavenly Father who will give me help when I ask. Maybe instead of focusing on all my shortcomings as a mother, I should be focusing on asking for more help from God. Praying and asking God to direct my thoughts and actions takes the burden off my shoulders. Because sometimes I don't understand what's going on with my children, but God does. And I can ask him for wisdom. I am so glad I am not alone, and neither are you.

Maybe you feel the same way. Perhaps you feel like you've let your children down today and made some mistakes. Let me encourage you that we can turn to God's word and find the truth and encouragement our hearts desperately need. Instead of focusing on perfection, we can rely on the Lord to help us endure all the things we face each day. And in protecting our children's hearts, trusting in God's promises for our families, hoping for the best for our kids, and persevering in the hard mothering moments, we are truly loving well.

With God's love in our hearts, and scripture as our guide, we can know how to love our families well. We are not alone in the daily demands of motherhood. **Our Heavenly Father wants to help us labor in love and run the race of motherhood with endurance.** And in the persevering we can allow God to shape our hearts and draw us nearer to himself.

So the next time you feel discouraged or tired in the daily labor of love, remind yourself that God wants perseverance over perfection. When you are overwhelmed in the labor and stretched to your limits, remember to ask God for his divine intervention and help. He is our ever present help in time of need and his love endures forever.

"Our Heavenly Father wants to help us labor in love and run the race of motherhood with endurance."

# 43

## WEEK
## FORTY-THREE

*BATTLE*

2 CORINTHIANS 7-8

2 CORINTHIANS 9-10

2 CORINTHIANS 11-12

2 CORINTHIANS 13, ROMANS 1

ROMANS 2, ACTS 20

**MEMORY VERSE**

"FINALLY, BE STRONG IN THE LORD AND IN HIS
MIGHTY POWER. PUT ON THE FULL ARMOR OF GOD,
SO THAT YOU CAN TAKE YOUR STAND AGAINST THE
DEVIL'S SCHEMES."

**EPHESIANS 6:10-11**

# THE BATTLE BELONGS TO HIM

**BY BRENNA KURZ**

At the beginning of 2022, I found out that I was pregnant!

Sadly, my joy faded quickly when a few short weeks later I was told that it would result in a miscarriage.

My heart was shattered as the waiting continued. I was so hopeful the Lord would make a way but it was not the way I would have chosen. I had complications that dragged it out longer than most and I was to the point where I just wanted the bad news to end.

I did the only things I knew to do, pray, hold tight to God's word and ask my community to come alongside me in prayer. While I felt the power of those prayers, I still struggled with intrusive thoughts. I was physically and mentally weak and vulnerable. I let my guard down and it was a green light for Satan to attack. Unfortunately, I did not see it right away.

Spiritual warfare is very real and we are up against it every single day as Christ followers. For me personally, I had never felt the fight so strongly. I sat night after night, tear after tear, trying to control the thoughts overwhelming my mind. So as I read, I was encouraged and felt seen by this timely message Paul shared about the war that we would not win with mere earlthy weapons.

He writes 2 Corinthians, to the church in Corinth. They were slandering his name and questioning his character, as Satan was doing to me. Paul reminded them to seek God's word and truth before they were deceived by all the lies. He states, "For though we live in this world, we do not wage war as the world does. The weapons we fight with are not the weapons of this world. On the contrary, they have divine power to demolish strongholds. We demolish arguments and every pretension that sets itself up against the knowledge of God, and we take captive every thought to make it obedient to Christ" (2 Cor. 10:3-5).

"God's truths embedded in our hearts prepares us for the battle!"

I needed this reminder, just as the Corinthians did. As I sat there and argued with Satan, I felt crazy but I could not give into the lies. Lies that I was not good enough, that something was wrong with me, and the flood of guilt for feeling the way I did when I should be standing confident on God's truths.

I knew what I had to do: suit up in the armor of God by "putting on the belt of truth, breastplate of righteousness, sandals with the gospel of peace, shield of faith, helmet of salvation and the sword of the Spirit, which is the word of God" (Eph. 6:14-17). I started praying, reciting scripture, blasting worship music and praying even more.

**God's truths embedded in our hearts prepares us for the battle!**

God comforted me during my time of need and reminded me that I was prepared for battle and He will do the same for you!

So, friend, no matter what you are going through, be ready when Satan comes to attack. Pray without ceasing and replace the lies with truth. Worship your way through it and seek your community that will help bear your burdens.

Put on the armor of God daily and He will prepare you for when the battles come. And take heart; He has already won the war!

# BETTER TOGETHER
*how community helps us grow*

**WE WEREN'T CREATED TO DO LIFE ALONE.**

God's design for us is that we be plugged into life-giving community.

At Rooted Moms, we define life-giving community as community where—
- There is genuine **connection** where each individual is seen, known, and loved.
- Individuals can give and receive **care** for physical, spiritual, and emotional needs.
- God's goodness is **celebrated** collectively.
- Time together serves as a **catalyst** for spiritual growth.

**HOW DOES STUDYING IN COMMUNITY CATALYZE SPIRITUAL GROWTH?**

- **Encouragement** | Growth is hard. Some weeks we will feel like we're running full speed, and other weeks we will feel like we're moving backwards. The trials that make us stronger can feel like they are crushing us instead. We need others on the outside looking into our lives to cheer us on so that we can continue to "press on toward the goal" (Phil. 3:14). Paul wrote to the church, "Therefore encourage one another and build each other up, just as in fact you are doing" (1 Thess. 5:11). Everyday life can tear us down but, in community, we can both give *and receive* encouragement to run our race well.

- **Accountability** | Have you ever started a Bible reading plan, only to abandon it 2 months, 2 weeks, or even 2 days in? How many times have you committed to stop a sinful behavior, then found yourself back in the same rut again? As Christ's body, we are called to hold each other accountable, as we are being transformed more into His image. In the context of community, we are able to "spur one another on toward love and good deeds" (Heb. 10:24).

- **Sharpening** | No two people are the same— we each have different personalities, passions, and perspectives. As we place ourselves in proximity to other believers, there will be times when we rub each other the wrong way. But that friction, when handled God's way, can be used for our good. Proverbs 27:17 says, "As iron sharpens iron, so one person sharpens another." Learn to lean into the tension, knowing that it is making you a more useful vessel for God's glory.

- **Strength |** There is something empowering about knowing we're not alone— that there are others fighting the good fight of faith alongside us, who have our back when the going gets tough. King Solomon observed, "Though one may be overpowered, two can defend themselves. A cord of three strands is not quickly broken" (Eccles. 4:12). Who do you have in your corner; who won't leave your side in the battle; who will wage war with you in prayer? Who can you do the same for? Community is a lot more than showing up to a building once a week. Engage with other believers and find that there is strength in numbers.

*Find your people.*

**Study with a friend**
Ask a friend to read through the Bible with you. Choose a plan and a start date, and make a commitment to follow through. Choose a friend who won't let you make excuses! Text one another with your daily takeaways and favorite observations. Share what stuck out to you most, and if there's an action you need to take. Meet at a coffee shop or have a video call to pray together regularly.

**Study with a group**
Get connected with a group at your church or start one of your own. Identify a day/time of the week you can set aside to meet consistently and decide where you will meet (online is a great option). Communicate the reading plan, and ask each participant to commit to study and attend as often as possible. For more practical tips on starting and leading a small group, visit www.rootedmoms.com/lead.

**Study with Rooted Moms**
Rooted Moms groups are online-based small groups of 5-10 women who meet regularly for the purpose of connecting and growing in their faith. Weekly discussion revolves around our year-round reading plan, which starts over in the Old Testament each September (enrollment is open year-round).

Our life-giving groups emphasize the biblical principles of connection, care, celebration and are a catalyst for spiritual growth. Rooted Moms groups are open to women from all different stages of life. We believe we have a lot to learn from one another— young adults, new moms, seasoned moms, empty nesters, and grandmas alike! Learn more and find your people at www.rootedmoms.com/community.

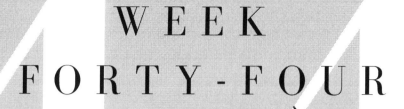

# WEEK
# FORTY-FOUR

## MINDSET

ROMANS 3-4

ROMANS 5-6

ROMANS 7-8

ROMANS 9-10

ROMANS 11-12

**MEMORY VERSE**

"THEREFORE NO ONE WILL BE DECLARED
RIGHTEOUS IN GOD'S SIGHT BY THE WORKS OF
THE LAW; RATHER, THROUGH THE LAW WE
BECOME CONSCIOUS OF OUR SIN."

**ROMANS 3:20**

# MIRRORS

## BY TAYLOR WATKINS

I used to look at the girl staring back at me in the mirror and say terrible things to her. Things I would never say to anyone else.

"Your body is ugly. Ugh, look at ALL those stretch marks EVERYWHERE. Come closer, look at these new wrinkles ... you look so old." I tore her to shreds because I couldn't believe she let herself get this way. With every harsh critique I plunged a knife deeper and deeper into her self confidence, killing it slowly.

In Romans, Paul talks about shifting our focus to the Holy Spirit that lies within us. He writes, "The mind governed by the flesh is death, but the mind governed by the Spirit is life and peace. The mind governed by the flesh is hostile to God; it does not submit to God's law, nor can it do so. Those who are in the realm of the flesh cannot please God" (Rom. 8:6-8).

Notice, Paul speaks about a mindset. He doesn't talk about actions that please God.

When we use only our actions to please God, but don't let Him in to renew our minds, we boil ourselves down to nothing but a religion. When you review your reflection on a surface level, you will easily be fooled. It is easy to appear clean on the outside, but it is far more complicated to have a well kept heart.
For example:
- You can sit in a church and your mind can be absent.
- You can read your Bible and not put the context into action.
- You can gossip without using a cuss word.

On the flip side, when we rest our eyes on the temptations of the world, we disregard God all together, finding no rest at all. You can't avoid the mirror and expect to avoid problems:
- "I don't want to feel convicted by my Bible, I'll read later."
- "I don't want to go to church because I have social anxiety. I'll try next week."
- "I know I'm really not supposed to ... but I really want to. I'll tell Jesus 'sorry' tomorrow."

Any of these thoughts sound familiar to you? Me too.

# "The mirror can be used as a tool instead of a judge."

The religious person looks in the mirror and likes what they see because they can't see any further. The procrastinator avoids the mirror afraid of what they might discover or have to change. What they both fail to realize is that no matter what person stands in front of the mirror, their reflections will always have one thing in common: sin.

We have a flesh mindset because we are sinful, but when we put our faith in God we can see through God's eyes.

So what is the point of the mirror? The point of the mirror is that it shows us where and how we need Jesus in our lives. **The mirror can be used as a tool instead of a judge.**

I abused the girl in the mirror for far too long. I had failed to mention how loved she was. It was when she stopped acknowledging me and turned to God, her confidence was resurrected.

"You are more than just a body." He said to her, "Your stretch marks are reminders of the two miracles I have given you and where you see wrinkles, I see growth." She felt alive again.

Who are you listening to when you look in the mirror? Today, dig into God's word without hesitation. Look at it with new eyes and ask God to search your heart. Remind yourself of the Holy Spirit that lives within you and draw near to Jesus for it is by Him we are saved.

# WEEK
# FORTY-FIVE

*SELF*

ROMANS 13-14

ROMANS 15-16

ACTS 21-22

ACTS 23-24

ACTS 25-26

**MEMORY VERSE**

"THOSE WHO BELONG TO CHRIST JESUS HAVE
CRUCIFIED THE FLESH WITH ITS PASSIONS AND
DESIRES. SINCE WE LIVE BY THE SPIRIT, LET US KEEP
IN STEP WITH THE SPIRIT."

**GALATIANS 5:24-25**

# NOT ABOUT ME

**BY LINDSAY MCNEELY**

Our family spent a glorious weekend with our closest friends in a cabin in the mountains recently. We have done this annually for the last decade. It is a joy to see how much our families have changed. Now our trips are filled with squeals and giggles from all of the little ones running around and playing. However, those giggles are often punctuated by yells, tattles, and tears. It is a joy to see our kids bond and grow together, but there are some growing pains as they navigate playing and conflict resolution.

Often we as parents spend time guiding our little ones as they run to tell us who did what, who took what, or how something is not fair. Their little minds and hearts are still very self-centered.

But can't we say the same?

Our culture and our world encourages us to focus on ourselves. We are bombarded with messages around self-care, growing ourselves, improving ourselves, and becoming our very best self. While these things are not necessarily bad, they can quickly replace the thing that is to be center - the person we were created to worship.

In the letter to the Romans, Paul shares what the life of a Christian should look like, and it is the opposite of what the world around us teaches. In Romans 13:14, Paul says, "Clothe yourselves with the Lord Jesus Christ, and do not think about how to gratify the desires of the flesh."

In the Christian life, we are to love our neighbor and consider them above ourselves. They may not do as we do, worship God as we worship God, or hold the same expectations that we hold, yet we are to respect our neighbors. Our goal as Christ-followers is not to please ourselves. It is to glorify God and love our neighbor well.

We can easily fall into the trap of self-glorification, especially in our social media driven world. I can quickly think that I deserve more, that I come first, and that my needs are the most important.

However, God calls us to so much more. He calls us to crucify our own desires so we can make room for His desires. When we let go of the things of our flesh, we can be filled with His Spirit, used for His kingdom, and shine His light for others to see.

**Jesus calls us to a countercultural life.** He made it clear in His ministry that choosing to follow Him requires sacrificing the things that we want and desire. Yet following Him is filled with promise and reward.

So how do we let go of these things of the flesh?

For me, it is coming to Jesus daily. When I spend regular time learning from His words and actions, the Holy Spirit brings them to mind just when I need them the most. Our flesh-pleasing desires come so naturally and easily, so I have found that I need to come before Jesus in prayer all throughout the day. When I am tempted to put me first, when my jealousy rears its head, or when I am tempted to act rashly out of my own desires, I find that if I can pause and come to God in prayer, even for just a quick second, it realigns my heart and mind with His.

To live the countercultural life that Christ calls you to, devote yourself to learning more about Him, spending quality time with Him in prayer, and joining Him in His work around you. He will meet you where you are and align your heart and mind to His.

"Jesus calls us to a countercultural life."

# WEEK
# FORTY-SIX

*TRUTH*

ACTS 27-28

COLOSSIANS 1-2

COLOSSIANS 3-4

PHILEMON

EPHESIANS 1-2

**MEMORY VERSE**

"BY THIS EVERYONE WILL KNOW THAT YOU ARE MY
DISCIPLES, IF YOU LOVE ONE ANOTHER."

**JOHN 13:35**

# AN UNCOMMON LOVE

**BY SARETTA WELLS**

I am blessed to have a husband that loves me well, but recently he did something that made me feel forgotten. In the past, I would have not said anything until later, when I would blow up over something small. This cycle brought guilt, and I knew He had to have a better way, so I began working on expressing my feelings with my husband as much as I do with my friends.

This vulnerability has led to intimacy and growth, so I was quick to pull him aside while our boys were playing. I wanted to share my feelings on how I perceived things even though I knew that he never intended to hurt me. I could see the recognition flow through his brain as he considered my words. He apologized, and we moved on with our day. What could have built into a major issue for me resolved in two minutes flat.

We see this mix of both truth and love in Paul's letter to the Colossians. He extended words of deep and meaningful praise and encouragement, but Paul also exhorted the Colossians toward truth, with the expressed goal that "they might be encouraged in heart and united in love" (Col. 2:2a). When Paul loved, he fought for people to have all the richness offered by a life with the Lord. He reminded them of the truth, warned against things that would draw them away, and pointed them toward Christ and unity. Paul's love wasn't fluff, and ours shouldn't be either.

The Colossians were a group of faithful believers that still had some kinks to work out, just like us. As part of the body of Christ, we have the same ability as Paul to strengthen one another and our relationships. If the truth will set us free, then we must be willing to share it with one another.

**Love does not exist without truth.** While this "truth in love" style of living isn't common in our culture, the Father has given us the truest definition of love through His Son, Jesus, and it is by this uncommon love that we will be recognized as His.

When we love others, sometimes we have to tell people hard things so that we can grow together. I have wasted a lot of time storing up hurts that were never intended. Maybe you can relate. I can know intent but still hold onto the hurt I felt over some issue like little bricks to make a wall between us.

As I've sought the Lord in how to handle my relationships, He challenged me to get honest with the people around me and stop trying to cover over things out of love and let love truly cover over all. The world tells us that we should forgive and move on, but that can lead us down a path of further struggle and pain if we never actually address our hurts. The Father, however, shows us a better way, combining grace and truth.

So next time you face a sticky situation with a friend or loved one, seek to handle it immediately so anger doesn't build and the relationship doesn't break, because one of the greatest acts of love is telling the truth.

"Love does not exist without truth."

# WEEK FORTY-SEVEN

## UNITY

EPHESIANS 3-4

EPHESIANS 5-6

PHILIPPIANS 1-2

PHILIPPIANS 3-4

HEBREWS 1-2

## MEMORY VERSE

"AS A PRISONER FOR THE LORD, THEN, I URGE YOU TO LIVE A LIFE WORTHY OF THE CALLING YOU HAVE RECEIVED. BE COMPLETELY HUMBLE AND GENTLE; BE PATIENT, BEARING WITH ONE ANOTHER IN LOVE, MAKING EVERY EFFORT TO KEEP THE UNITY OF THE SPIRIT THROUGH THE BOND OF PEACE."

**EPHESIANS 4:1-3**

# COMMUNICATION IS KEY

**BY BRITTANY MARLOW**

My first daughter was a terrible sleeper. While trying to keep my eyelids propped open and a baby from falling out of my arms, my husband snored happily one room over. It infuriated me.

Why didn't he offer to change her diaper when I had just done it? Didn't he hear her crying in the middle of the night? Why didn't he offer to make dinner every now and then? My anger would build all night until both my daughter and I drifted off to sleep. Why couldn't he just do these things?

I wanted him to know exactly how to help me and to know exactly what I needed, when I needed it. How could I expect him to know when and how I needed help if I wasn't being clear? I realized I wasn't asking for his help and when he did offer, I wouldn't let him. We needed to be working together but guess who was hindering that? I'll tell you right now, it wasn't him. We weren't united as one because I was dividing us.

In Paul's letter to the Ephesians, he explains to them to "live worthy of the calling they have received" (Eph. 4:1) and to do so with humility, making every effort to stay peacefully unified. Paul later relates this concept to marriage: that as man and wife you should be unified "as one flesh" (Eph. 5:31).

After reading this, I felt called out, rightfully so. In the struggle, I was looking to myself to do everything when I should have been looking to God who would have pointed me to my husband. I was trying my best to live out my calling of being a mother, but I wasn't putting the same effort into my calling of being a wife. I wasn't humbling myself or submitting myself to my husband, so how could I expect any sort of peace?

I was sitting in that chair at night wishing my daughter would sleep better or that my husband would read my mind. Instead, I should have been communicating with God on how I could communicate better to my husband. It was easier for the enemy to attack me in my sleep deprived state, feeling alone and upset, because I was cutting myself off from God's guidance and my husband's support.

"Live worthy of your calling and humble yourself to allow others to live worthy of theirs."

God doesn't want us to do everything ourselves. The Bible explains that we are all part of the body of Christ with different functions and to be able to function properly, we have to work together (1 Cor. 12:12-28).

We need our brain to tell our feet to move forward so we can walk. In this way, we need our communication to help our families work as a cohesive unit. When we fail to communicate, it is easier for negativity and resentment to bubble to the surface. The doubts and anger from the enemy start to seep in. Paul encourages the Ephesians to "speak the truth [and not to] give the devil an opportunity" (Eph. 4:25-27).

If you're feeling alone and unsupported, maybe it's because you've cut yourself off from the other parts of the body within your support system. By not communicating the truth of your feelings and needs, you rob your support system of living within the calling that God has given them. **Live worthy of your calling and humble yourself to allow others to live worthy of theirs.**

In the quiet moments (and the loud ones), I encourage you to pray fervently. After all, communication is key. Let God's grace and gentle guidance lead you to those around you when you need help and encouragement. Submit to your spouse in love and respect, and feel the peaceful unity God has graced upon both of you.

# 48

## WEEK FORTY-EIGHT

### REST

HEBREWS 3-4

HEBREWS 5-6

HEBREWS 7-8

HEBREWS 9-10

HEBREWS 11-12

**MEMORY VERSE**

"THERE REMAINS, THEN, A SABBATH-REST FOR THE PEOPLE OF GOD; FOR ANYONE WHO ENTERS GOD'S REST ALSO RESTS FROM THEIR WORKS, JUST AS GOD DID FROM HIS."

**HEBREWS 4:9-10**

# REST IN FAITH

**BY DANA SCHAEFER**

As I finished the last section of the test, my brain hurt, my eyes were heavy with sleep, and I wanted nothing more than to rest my head on the table. I struggled to complete the National Counselor Exam (NCE) required for my state licensure.

I studied for months after completing my degree and fieldwork for this test. I studied with colleagues and my husband, who quizzed me using flashcards. I took several practice tests to improve my familiarity with the test format. I even bought a test prep course off the Internet and worked my way through it. In short, I had done everything right to prepare for this test except for one thing—rest.

The test was given at a testing center a couple of hours from my home. So I made a hotel reservation, packed my suitcase, and headed out with excitement and anticipation. I arrived at the hotel, settled into the room, and went out to treat myself to a steak dinner. When I returned from the restaurant, I thought, "Let me do a little refresher."

I opened my study guide, pulled out my flashcards, and started cramming. Minutes turned into hours, and the daylight faded into night. Nevertheless, I kept on cramming. I did not believe that my careful, methodical preparation was enough to help me pass the test. My unbelief robbed me of adequate rest.

Have you ever spent a sleepless night tossing and turning because swirling, anxious thoughts kept you from drifting off? Maybe you can think of a similar time when your unbelief or lack of faith kept you from getting the rest you needed.

Hebrews 4:1 explains, "Therefore, since the promise of entering his rest still stands, let us be careful that none of you be found to have fallen short of it."

This good news comes with a sober warning: God's rest is available! But you can miss it too. The type of rest that the writer of Hebrews is talking about is a literal repose. It is not a euphemism for death or the afterlife; according to Strong's Concordance its literal Greek translation (katapausis) indicates a cessation from work.*

*The Interlinear Bible: Hebrew - Greek - English. Jay P. Green, translator, Hendrickson. 2011.

# "Faith in God's promises produces rest."

Hebrews 4:2 repeats the promise and warning, "For we also have had the good news proclaimed to us, just as they did; but the message they heard was of no value to them, because they did not share the faith of those who obeyed." Whenever a principle in Scripture repeats, it is important! Back-to-back these verses teach that the same promise of rest was made, yet one group did not combine what they heard with faith. **Faith in God's promises produces rest.**

A few hours into my evening cramming, I realized that I needed to stop studying and rest. Even though I finished the exam exhausted, I passed the test the next day! My one regret from that situation is that I should have activated my faith in the careful preparation I made for the test. My unbelief and self-doubt robbed me of the rest I needed. I learned that rest is necessary to do my best at whatever task I face.

The author reminds us in Hebrews 4:4 that after a busy week of creation, God himself rested on the seventh day. If God instituted the pattern for regular rest periods, shouldn't we as women take his lead? What keeps women from entering into rest? Could it be unbelief or self-doubt? Do you believe that if you stopped serving, cleaning, teaching, cooking, and working, your household would crash down around you? Is your constant busyness a symptom of unbelief?

If it is, Hebrews has good news. Mix a little faith with the promise God has extended to you. Rest for a minute. God has offered you rest; take him up on it!

# WEEK FORTY-NINE

*SINCERITY*

1 TIMOTHY 1-2

1 TIMOTHY 3-4

1 TIMOTHY 5-6

2 TIMOTHY 1-2

2 TIMOTHY 3-4

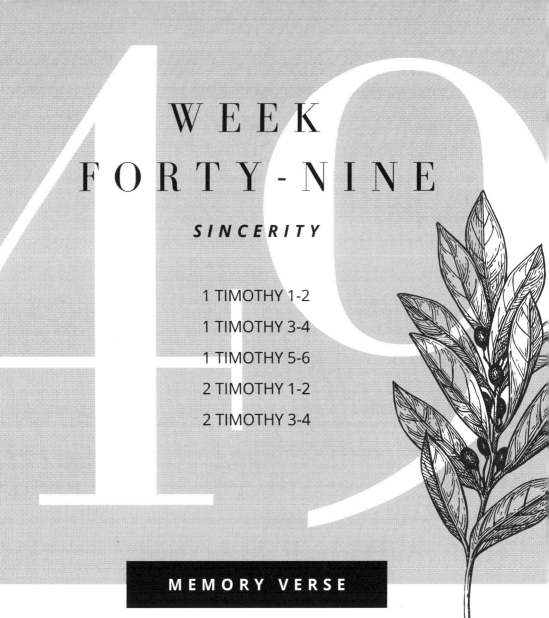

## MEMORY VERSE

"I HAVE BEEN CRUCIFIED WITH CHRIST AND I NO LONGER LIVE, BUT CHRIST LIVES IN ME. THE LIFE I NOW LIVE IN THE BODY, I LIVE BY FAITH IN THE SON OF GOD, WHO LOVED ME AND GAVE HIMSELF FOR ME."

**GALATIANS 2:20**

# LIVING FAITH

**BY KATIE GIBSON**

The more anxious I am about something, the more I tend to overcomplicate it. For instance...

- If I am nervous about a meeting, I'll try to curate a new outfit from pieces in my closet instead of grabbing something I already know coordinates.
- If I am anxious about a very full schedule, I'll throw more tasks into the mix instead of postponing things that can wait.
- If I am anxious about having a large crowd of people over to my house, I plan an elaborate menu instead of something simple.

Don't ask me why I do these things (my therapist would probably have an explanation). And when it comes to my history of overcomplicating things, parenting is no exception.

I remember, when my kids were little, being so anxious about getting everything just right. I wanted (and still want) them to walk with Christ more than anything, so I got busy overcomplicating....

- I read a plethora of Christian parenting books... which left me feeling like a *failure.*
- I started daily devotionals with my toddlers... which left me *frustrated.*
- I tried to monitor everything they watched and did with perfect precision... and it left me *fatigued.*

My Bible told me that Jesus' yoke was easy and His burden was light (Matt. 11:30), but that truth didn't line up with my experience of feeling like a chronically frustrated, fatigued, failing Christian parent. Maybe, under the surface, you've been feeling the same tension.

Maybe you, too, are exhausted from constant striving and overcomplicating. How do we raise children who grow to love and follow Christ organically, without all the fuss?

In Paul's latter letters, we meet Timothy, a young faith-filled minister. While we don't learn much about his personal life, we do get a glimpse of how Timothy came to a personal relationship with God. Paul writes, "I am reminded of your sincere faith, which first lived in your grandmother Lois and in your mother Eunice and, I am persuaded, now lives in you also" (2 Tim. 1:5).

At some point (possibly on one of Paul's earlier journeys to Lystra) Lois and Eunice had put their faith in Christ. But they didn't just relegate Jesus to Sundays, or their quiet times — their faith was deep and genuine, so much so that the outer working of it infiltrated every area of their lives.

The power of a mom's or grandmother's influence cannot be overstated. Their example had such an impact on the young man that Timothy grew to know and follow Jesus himself. *Their living faith lived on in him.*

While there's no way to guarantee salvation for our own children, we can be "salt and light" to them by living out a genuine (unfeigned) faith. The pressure is off, friends— we don't have to be anxious, strive, and overcomplicate.

**As moms, our job is to remain rooted in Christ, and let the fruit attract others.** A life overflowing with the presence and goodness of God is simply irresistible. How do we live out sincere faith?

Here are a few examples of what that looks like in my life:
- Asking God for help, then celebrating and recording when God answers.
- Admitting my sin and apologizing to my children when I lose my temper.
- Serving and being connected to the body of Christ through our local church.
- Making and taking dinner to a family who is going through hardship.

Today, ask God to reveal any anxiety you're carrying about your children, and any ways you may be overcomplicating. Release your kids to the Lord, knowing He loves them and has good plans for them. While devotionals and parenting books are good tools, we don't have to stress and strive. Our kids don't need our perfection, they need us to show them what living faith looks like.

"As moms, our job is to remain rooted in Christ, and let the fruit attract others."

# 50

## WEEK FIFTY
### *TESTIMONY*

TITUS 1-3

1 PETER 1-2

1 PETER 3-4

1 PETER 5, 2 PETER 1

2 PETER 2-3

**MEMORY VERSE**

"...ALWAYS BE PREPARED TO GIVE AN ANSWER TO EVERYONE WHO ASKS YOU TO GIVE THE REASON FOR THE HOPE THAT YOU HAVE...."

**1 PETER 3:15**

# YOUR TODAY TESTIMONY

**BY JOAN LAVORI**

It was 12:20 pm. Another 10 minutes, and the meeting would be over. Our Bible Study leadership team was having its weekly after-study meeting. This was a part of the ongoing training that we participated in during the year. This week's topic was how to share your testimony. "Oh no!" I groaned inwardly, "not my favorite topic." This was not something I ever felt comfortable doing. I sank in my seat, unwilling to volunteer and hoping I would not be called on to share.

The leader spoke about how we can take a broader view of our personal testimony. I thought about what she was saying and realized that she was right. My struggles with sin did not go away once I accepted Christ as my savior. As a matter of fact, they probably increased. I have faced situations that tested my faith and made me question if I really had a relationship with Christ.

As I grew in faith by feasting on God's Word, I was drawn closer to Christ. Victory over sin is a testimony I could share. It is not the "accepting Jesus Christ as my savior" testimony, but it's a testimony of what He is doing in our lives today; our "Today Testimony" is the evidence of Godly living.

In 1 Peter 3, the apostle is writing to Christians about Godly living. He tells wives to submit to their husbands and husbands to love their wives, according to their God-given roles. Wives are to obey because God commands them to, and husbands will find their prayers hindered if they dishonor their wives. Peter encourages his brethren to love each other, be compassionate, humble, and to turn from evil and do good.

Verse 17 of 1 Peter 3 tells us, "It is better, if it is God's will, to suffer for doing good than for doing evil." The challenge for these believers was to respond in love, even if they should suffer for doing what was right. Living in exile, as aliens in a foreign land, they were facing daily persecution because of their faith in Christ. Despite the hardships they were facing, the way they lived their lives was a testimony to those around them. Each day, they could share a testimony with others of how and why they lived as they did, a "Today Testimony." Their "Today Testimony" could lead to sharing their saving testimony.

"A Today Testimony is built on a Saving Testimony."

Jesus hung on the cross to save us all, but He, too, began with a "Today Testimony" as He prayed, "Father forgive them for they do not know what they are doing" (Luke 23:34). This led to one of the criminals who hung beside Him being saved that day (Luke 23:40-43). Because of Jesus' example, we can share our "Today Testimony" with others.

**A Today Testimony is built on a Saving Testimony.**

Have you ever struggled with sharing your testimony? Does telling your whole story seem too daunting? Then, how about sharing your "Today Testimony?"

God is at work in your life every day, in small ways and in great ways. When your little one has a meltdown at the playground and you are able to hug him despite your anger and embarrassment, credit God for giving you patience. When you can joyfully celebrate the birth of your best friend's fifth child, despite your fourth miscarriage and your still empty arms, credit the joy to your growing faith and trust in a sovereign God.

Your "Today Testimony" could lead someone to accept Jesus as their Lord and Savior. What an awesome privilege that would be!

# 5 WEEK FIFTY-ONE

## CONFESSION

JUDE, 1 JOHN 1

1 JOHN 2-3

1 JOHN 4-5

2 JOHN, 3 JOHN

REVELATION 1-2

## MEMORY VERSE

"THEREFORE, IF ANYONE IS IN CHRIST, THE
NEW CREATION HAS COME: THE OLD HAS GONE,
THE NEW IS HERE!"

2 CORINTHIANS 5:17

# FLIRTING WITH SIN

**BY KERYN STOKES**

When I moved out of my parents house at the age of 18 years old, there wasn't a substance I wouldn't try if it was offered to me. There wasn't a party I wouldn't attend, or most often, I was the one hosting!

At times, the words that came out of my mouth were unbecoming to say the least. The actions I made were even worse. Yet all the while, I would proudly tell others "yes, I'm a Christian!" when they saw the Christian-fish tattooed on my wrist.

My hypocrisy and disregard for Christ would finally catch up with me in the way of legal trouble. It was in a conversation with my mother where I was presented with the reality of what I'd let my life become when it all hit me. She said something along the lines of, "this is what happens when you flirt with sin." *Ouch, she was right.*

Confronted with the illicit relationship between my rampant sin and self-proclaimed Christianity, I knew the two could not coexist. My sin was like an oil that does not mix with the living water that is God. This metaphor is true for sin of any size or stature, sin simply is not of God. We cannot carelessly let sin rule our lives and claim to be in fellowship with Christ, we must align our lives to His.

As I read this week's scriptures, I couldn't help but feel convicted. John is addressing heretical teachers that were within the church making false claims regarding Christianity. They claimed to be in-step with God, even partnering with Him, but they lived immorally. They rejected the notion that they were sinful by nature and they denied that their sin was displeasing to God!

My jaw dropped over the simple truths such as "Everyone who sins breaks the law; in fact, sin is lawlessness" (1 John 3:4) and "If we claim to have fellowship with Him and yet walk in the darkness, we lie and do not live out the truth" (1 John 1:6).

In 1 John 1:9, John writes "If we confess our sins, He is faithful and just and will forgive us our sins and purify us from all unrighteousness." Confession in its simplest terms is to agree with God. **Confession is the cure for sinfulness.**

The first change I enacted in my life was that of confession to God and to those I had wronged or led astray. I encourage you today to confess your sins to our Father who is faithful and just to forgive so that He could cleanse you from all your unrighteousness that you could become a new creation in Him (2 Cor. 5:17). Your first prayer of confession can be as simple as, "Lord, I agree I have lived sinfully." May the words cross your heart before they cross your lips.

Take every new day and each new endeavor with one foot in front of the other, fully relying on God's strength. With every step in the right direction aligned with Christ, you will become the woman and new creation God destined you to be!

"Confession is the cure for sinfulness."

# WEEK FIFTY-TWO

## WORTHY

REVELATION 3-4

REVELATION 5, 7

REVELATION 12, 18

REVELATION 19-20

REVELATION 21-22

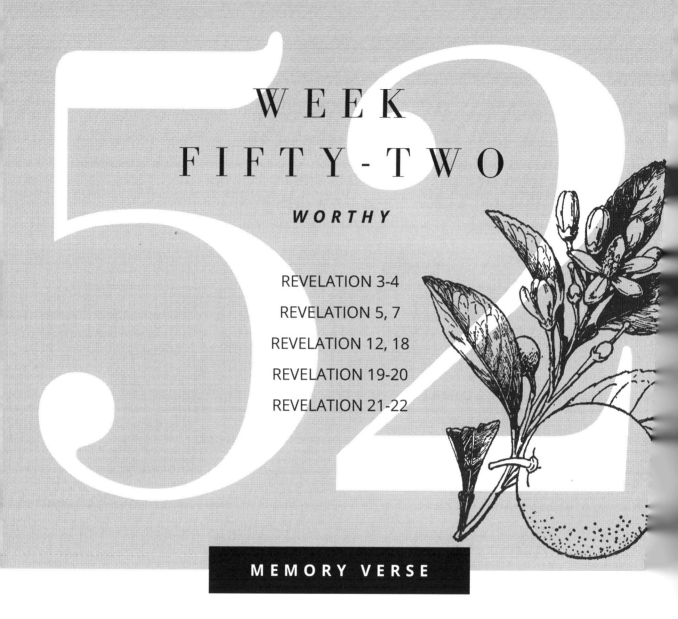

## MEMORY VERSE

"AND THEY SANG A NEW SONG, SAYING: "YOU ARE WORTHY TO TAKE THE SCROLL AND TO OPEN ITS SEALS, BECAUSE YOU WERE SLAIN, AND WITH YOUR BLOOD YOU PURCHASED FOR GOD PERSONS FROM EVERY TRIBE AND LANGUAGE AND PEOPLE AND NATION."

**REVELATION 5:9**

# WORTHY IS THE LAMB

**BY FAITH SPEARMAN**

I remember being a child, sitting in church hearing about Revelation, and then later on as a teenager reading it for myself and, in my lack of clarity, being afraid.

All I saw was there would be a cost; a cost that's the result of living in a world that desperately needs Jesus. A world where we are called to be in it but not "of it," simultaneously sharing the gospel while keeping the expectations of society at throwing distance. But at the time, I shied away from it, unsure of the worth that I so plainly see now.

Recently, I had another opportunity to be afraid. I was facing ridicule and persecution at my job for standing in a faith that my boss deemed "ridiculous" and "politically incorrect," and in my momentary fear of what could happen as a result of defending my faith, I almost let that same faith lapse. But in that suspended moment, I heard so clearly in my Spirit what I already knew to be the truth: "He's worth it."

Every time I read Revelation now, all I'm reminded of is how worthy He really is. He is worth the discomfort or the ridicule. He is worthy of lifting me His name, even, and especially, in the midst of the valleys.

In reading Revelation, John speaks of Jesus' worthiness. He writes, "He is worthy to take the scroll and open that seal" (Rev. 5:9, 12). When John attests to Jesus being worthy to open the seal, think of it as the scroll being a Holy letter addressed to Jesus alone, being the only One worthy of opening it. He alone was worthy of opening this Holy scroll because He alone died on the cross so that you and I might live!

He alone is so worthy that every creature in heaven, on earth, under the earth, and on the sea will proclaim, "To him who sits on the throne and to the Lamb be praise and honor and glory and power, for ever and ever!" (Rev. 5:13). How appropriate that worth is such a hot topic these days: how much is land worth? A home? Fuel? Milk and eggs? How much is my career worth in comparison to my family, even my faith? What is it that made Jesus worthy?

With worth, there's usually a cost and Jesus's cost for worthiness was death. The painful trade of blood for:

- Our salvation.
- Our righteousness.
- Our freedom.
- Our eternal life.
- Us to obtain all that falls under the Kingdom of Heaven.

Friends, be encouraged in that when you come face to face with the nature of this world, praise Him anyway. When you find persecution in the workplace, or discomfort in standing alone in your faith, be reminded of His worth. Be reminded that He faced not only ridicule, slander and persecution, but death, and was victorious. The victory that made a way for you and I to know what it is to openly step into that secret place found in unhindered, genuine worship, and find that same victory.

**Praise Him for paying the price of being our worthy sacrifice even while we were still in the valley.** Praising Him anyway because we can know that perseverance breeds faithfulness and "...faithfulness breeds righteousness" (Rom. 1:17).

He paid it all with His blood. So be heartened to return that sacrifice with praise, no matter what the valley looks like, because HE is worthy; because He is always faithful, even in our faithlessness, bringing us, every time, from the valley to the mountain top.

"Praise Him for paying the price of being our worthy sacrifice even while we were still in the valley."

# CELEBRATE

*You did it, friend.*

You didn't just read the Bible in a year— *you became more rooted in Christ.*

Your trust has deepened.
You are more joyful and peace-filled.
You are wiser and spiritually stronger than ever before.
You are holding your head a little higher...

How do we know? Because that's what happens when you get in God's Word.

Today, as you end this year-long adventure, take a moment to celebrate all that God has done. Go back and read your "note to self" (pg. 8), and recognize God's faithfulness. Did He meet you at your level of expectation? It is likely He *exceeded* it.

Remember early on in the Israelites' journey how they would place stones to remember the great things God had done? Consider the next two pages your "stones." Take a few minutes to reflect and write your testimony of what God has done in your heart and life over the past 52 weeks, as you've pressed on to know Him more.

_____
_____
_____
_____
_____
_____
_____
_____
_____
_____
_____
_____
_____

# *WHAT NOW?*

Throughout our study, we've emphasized that reading the Bible isn't meant to be a checklist item, but a lifelong journey of knowing God and becoming more deeply rooted in Him.

If you're wondering, "What now?" here are a few ways you can continue to fuel your hunger for God's Word, and continue to grow in this next season.

### READ IT AGAIN.

Yep, that's right. We think you should read the Bible all over again. Why? Because unlike other books we read once and stick on a shelf, God's Word is "alive and active" (Heb. 4:12) and speaks to us in different ways in different seasons. You will be amazed at the new perspectives God will show you through the same stories.

Our Rooted Moms community reads through the Bible every year, and we would love for you to join us. If you liked the "Rooted" format, we publish a new volume each year with all-new devotionals, memory verses and resources! Learn more and purchase a copy at www.rootedmoms.com/rooted.

### DIG DEEPER WITH A BOOK STUDY.

Was there a book of the Bible or specific story you longed to slow down and spend more time on? Chances are you can find a book study. Online Christian book retailers carry some great options. Here are a few of our team's recommendations:
- *"Elijah"* by Priscilla Shirer (study of Elijah)
- *"Trustworthy"* by Lysa Terkeurst (study of 1 and 2 Kings)
- *"Better"* by Jen Wilkin (study of Hebrews)

### CHOOSE A TOPICAL STUDY.

Throughout the past year, you may have recognized some areas of weakness in your walk. Maybe you are struggling with an addiction, or pride, or simply long for a more consistent prayer life. The Bible app (by YouVersion) offers a plethora of FREE studies on nearly every topic under the sun! Download the app and utilize the search feature to find one to help you grow in victory in a specific area.

# CONNECT
# WITH US

## ROOTED MOMS MINISTRIES

 WWW.ROOTEDMOMS.COM

 FACEBOOK.COM/ROOTEDMOMS

 @ROOTEDMOMS

 PINTEREST.COM/ROOTEDMOMS

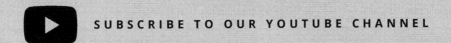 SUBSCRIBE TO OUR YOUTUBE CHANNEL

LIKE, FOLLOW, AND SUBSCRIBE FOR RESOURCES, COMMUNITY,
AND ENCOURAGEMENT TO HELP YOU STAY ROOTED.

Made in the USA
Columbia, SC
26 August 2022

66110734R00133